UP TO OUR EYEBALLS

UP TO OUR EYEBALLS

How Shady Lenders and Failed
Economic Policies Are
Drowning Americans in Debt

José García, James Lardner, and Cindy Zeldin

With assistance from Myra Batchelder
and Jennifer Wheary

Published in collaboration with Demos

THE NEW PRESS

NEW YORK
LONDON

Requests for permission to reproduce selections from this book should be mailed to: Permissions Department, The New Press, 38 Greene Street, New York, NY 10013.

Published in the United States by The New Press, New York, 2008
Distributed by W. W. Norton & Company, Inc., New York

LIBRARY OF CONGRSS CATALOGING-IN-PUBLICATION DATA

García, José, 1975–
Up to our eyeballs : how shady lenders and failed economic policies are drowning
Americans in debt / José García, James Lardner, and Cindy Zeldin.
p. cm.
Includes bibliographical references.
ISBN 978-1-59558-211-9 (hbk.)
1. Debt—United States.   2. Consumer credit—United States.
3. Financial services industry—United States.   I. Lardner, James.
II. Zeldin, Cindy.   III. Title.
HG3756.U54G37 2008
332.70973—dc22

2007043894

The New Press was established in 1990 as a not-for-profit alternative to the large, commercial publishing houses currently dominating the book publishing industry. The New Press operates in the public interest rather than for private gain, and is committed to publishing, in innovative ways, works of educational, cultural, and community value that are often deemed insufficiently profitable.

www.thenewpress.com

A Caravan book.
For more information, visit www.caravanbooks.org.

Composition by dix!
This book was set in Minion

Printed in the United States of America

2   4   6   8   10   9   7   5   3   1

CONTENTS

FOREWORD

DEBT. The word alone causes people's blood pressure to rise. It's a hard-sounding word, phonetically in sync with its impact on people's lives. The presence of over five hundred Debtors Anonymous chapters across the country indicates that, for many people, being in debt signifies a disease they can't seem to control. The personal finance industry—and it is now surely an industry—generates thousands of books, television programs, and radio shows, all aimed at helping people reclaim their lives from debt peonage and get on the path to financial salvation. Viewers of late-night television are bombarded with commercials promising quick and easy ways to get out of debt. Debt collection is one of the fastest growing occupations in the United States today.

Helping people get out of debt has become big business. The private sector, from radio and television networks to publishing houses, has grasped the enormity of the nation's personal debt crisis, creating an abundance of products that promise to help people reclaim control over their financial lives. Most of these follow the predictable pedagogy of "spend less, save more," the parallel of the "just say no" advice that did nothing to win the war on drugs. But people embrace this approach because it taps into the values of self-reliance and self-empowerment. People like to feel in control of their lives—to feel that, ultimately, they are responsible for whether their fiscal ledger is red or black.

The rapid growth in the amount of debt the average American has been accumulating—from credit cards, mortgages, payday loans, student loans, and various other sources—hasn't been treated as an economic issue worthy of national attention by our media or our elected officials. No matter that in one generation the average mortgage payment for the typical middle-class family has nearly doubled, or that credit card debt grew from an average of $518 per household in 1980 to $7,519 in 2003.[1] Or that each year roughly 15 million families take out payday loans, which typically charge an annual percentage rate (APR) of 400 percent, costing them about $3.4 billion in fees and interest.[2] As far as most journalists and politicians are concerned, rising debt is a personal problem best dealt with through belt tightening and financial education. Meanwhile, the real story about why more and more households are caught in the debt vise remains untold, even as record numbers of families fall into financial collapse.

But the real story is starting to leak out. This story acknowledges the economic bind most households now find themselves in, with rising costs for everything from housing to health care and incomes that haven't kept up or have even declined. The real story also acknowledges the lending industry's role in this mess. Set free by two decades of deregulation, today's creditors have cooked up products that are so complicated, deceptive, and trap-laden that even the most sophisticated borrowers can't tell a good loan from a bad one. This is the story that *Up to Our Eyeballs* dares to tell, tracking both the economic and the political forces that are responsible for our debt crisis. It is a story that has finally begun to penetrate the nation's consciousness.

In 2007, as homeowners began defaulting on their subprime loans and billions of dollars of mortgage-backed securities began going bad, suddenly the lack of vigorous oversight and responsible lending standards became a national concern. The fact that millions of families were losing their most personal possession— their homes—was treated as a lesser story. While Wall Street's penchant for these high-risk mortgage-backed securities had helped fuel the rapid growth and aggressive marketing of sub- prime adjustable-rate mortgages, the very same investors became much less enamored when the duplicitous tactics used to peddle the mortgages to desperate homeowners resulted in hundreds of thousands of loans that couldn't be repaid. That, more than the duping of American homeowners, finally captured the attention of the media and the politicians.

The other meltdown that captured the nation's attention oc- curred in the student loan industry. An investigation initiated by the New York State attorney general's office, uncovered all the ele- ments of a good scandal in this seemingly sleepy business. It turns out that the nation's biggest student lenders—which receive siz- able subsidies from the federal government to participate in the federal student loan program—were providing kickbacks and other incentives to college financial aid administrators in order to buy their way onto preferred provider lists, assuring them of a high proportion of student loans on those campuses.

The unraveling of the subprime mortgage market and the growing scandal involving student loan companies have helped illuminate the debt problem as something a bit more complicated than the loosening of moral constraints around spending. There are larger economic and political forces at work, forces that include lax or negligent oversight and accountability of lenders in an era of deregulation, as well as a growing demand for credit as households face untenable choices in a new economic order that has them grappling with greater risk and less security.

The economic and social conditions that once allowed most individuals in this country to live largely debt-free (except for a mortgage and a car payment) no longer hold. Americans' economic security has declined and our public structures have decayed. Today individuals are as likely to go into credit card debt for an abscessed tooth as for a flat-screen television. Young people today are taking on huge levels of debt in order to finance their college education, something that was unheard-of a generation ago. And as incomes for all but the wealthiest have fallen or remained flat, a new type of loan—the payday loan—has been created for those times when there's too much month left at the end of the paycheck.

At the same time that Americans' paychecks were growing weaker, either in absolute terms or relative to their expenses, the financial industry was undergoing rapid changes as well. Deregulation and technological change opened up new markets for credit, fueling a rapid expansion of lending. Credit cards, which were once the province of those with middle and higher incomes, now were available to lower-income individuals. A bevy of new mortgage products helped families stretch to buy homes in overheated markets, even without any money down. But along with those real innovations that benefited many came the rise of referee-free lending. Rules that once protected consumers were relaxed, or replaced with rules that benefited lenders to the detriment of consumers. As lending underwent a technological revolution, enforcement grew antiquated and oversight grew increasingly lax. The stoic, stable lending industry of my parents' generation morphed into a hyperaggressive, no-holds-barred marketing machine designed to generate profits by obscuring the real costs of using its products and building in booby traps like balloon payments, prepayment penalties, and universal default to keep those in the grip of debt from ever breaking free.

Without deregulation, the balance sheet of most households would likely look very different today. And in all likelihood, so would their lives. Access to credit of all forms provided households with a much-needed relief valve to deal with the fundamental economic shifts that often significantly challenged their ability to make ends meet. Debt also became the way to deal with a decaying public safety net that no longer caught those who lost their jobs or their health insurance. And debt has also been the answer to skyrocketing tuition prices as federal financial aid has grown anemic and state support of higher education has all but made it a private responsibility rather than a public one.

So, why aren't Americans outraged?

Individuals who've been duped, deceived, or just plain ripped off will speak with passion about a rigged system that needs to be fixed, but their outrage remains isolated: millions of individual complaints and abuses haven't added up to a public outcry. Instead, it's dampened, if not entirely stamped out, by the notion that getting into debt, and stumbling under its weight, is a *personal* problem. It's something for financial guru Suze Orman or the wildly popular personal finance radio host Dave Ramsey to help us straighten out, not something we as a society should grapple with. On top of the very personal way we think about debt, there's another not so minor obstacle: many of our nation's leaders have a real stake in maintaining the status quo. Standing up to the interests of the lending industry would mean looking a gift horse in the mouth. There are at best a dozen members of Congress who are willing to upset the banking lobby, but the majority—on both sides of the aisle—have chosen to keep their seats and their perks and let the American people fend for themselves. Whether because of the influence of money or the belief that indebted individuals deserve what they get, our elected officials have chosen to stand by silently as students get taken for a ride, seniors get duped into refinance deals that cost them their homes, and low-income neighborhoods get walloped by payday lenders and unscrupulous "buy here, pay here" car lots.

Up to Our Eyeballs should be a wake-up call for our nation's leaders that the status quo is neither economically sustainable nor morally defensible. The book was written by three colleagues who work on issues of economic opportunity and security. Demos, a nonpartisan public policy research and advocacy organization, has studied the issue of rising debt for several years, publishing nearly a dozen reports on the subject. It's a problem from which few have been immune. But over the years, as more and more households find themselves borrowing to make ends meet and then further squeezed by deceptive and abusive lending terms, there has been little progress. In 2007 Congress held numerous hearings on a range of lending issues, and committee members used tough language to describe the behavior of the lenders brought in to testify before them, threatening them with the stick of legislation if they didn't clean up their act. But despite the tough veneer of the hearings, it's still business as usual.

We hope that this book, along with the ongoing efforts of our colleagues who stand up for the rights of consumers, will help spark a national debate that will address the growing problem of families who are losing their homes because of predatory lending, young people who are overwhelmed by student debt, households who are relying on credit cards to keep the lights on and food in the fridge, and the common thread that weaves their stories together: economic vulnerability and the deregulated lending industry designed to exploit it.

—Tamara Draut

1

BORROWING TO MAKE ENDS MEET

IT'S *SATURDAY NIGHT LIVE,* and Chris Parnell is a financial management guru with a unique new program for staying out of debt: First you make the money. Then you spend it.

Confusion is writ large across the faces of his would-be pupils, hyperconsumers Amy Poehler and Steve Martin. So, says Poehler, you check your bank account before you buy something?

Right, says Parnell.

But what if you don't have the money, Martin wants to know. Then how do you buy it?

Parnell refers them to his book. It's called *Don't Buy Stuff You Cannot Afford.* Order now, and he'll throw in a free copy of the companion volume, *Seriously, If You Don't Have the Money, Don't Buy It.*[1]

The book titles may be over the top, but the message is painfully familiar: America has become a nation of spendthrifts, running out to buy giant-screen TVs and Jacuzzis because the neighbors did. Extravagance leads to debt. Debt leads to trouble. This simple morality tale, reverberating through a multitude of self-help books and articles, has become the standard explanation of our nation's debt woes. But it doesn't add up.

Are some of us spending money we don't have on things we don't need? Absolutely. Does that fact explain the more than $2 trillion of household debt that American families are carrying?[2] Not even remotely. In fact, a typical American family spends less today on so-called consumables (furniture, clothing, appliances) than its counterpart of a generation ago. The big spending increases have come in the "unavoidables"—transportation, energy, and the three h's: health care, higher education, and housing.[3] The places where we spend more turn out to be where we borrow more, too.

Health care costs, for example, are increasing at a much faster clip than workers' earnings or overall inflation. So it's easy to see why more and more people are using credit cards to pay for doctor visits and hospital procedures. Medical expenses are part of the story for about a third of low- and middle-income families who carry credit card debt, and they're the families who owe the most—an average of $11,623 per household in one recent survey, compared to $7,964 for those who had not used credit cards for medical purposes.[4]

Higher education is on a similar track, with costs rising sharply and more of the burden falling directly on college students and their families. Two-thirds of all students now graduate with student loan debt; the average is over $19,000.[5] Many are still making payments ten or fifteen years later. Today, one out of five college students ends up with debt—and without a diploma.[6] More than half use credit cards to pay for textbooks and supplies, which come to about a quarter of the cost of tuition and fees at a typical four-year public institution.[7]

Housing costs have also skyrocketed, as few Americans have failed to notice. In the early 1970s, a year's worth of mortgage payments added up to $5,820 (in inflation-adjusted dollars) for the average middle-class family; by 2006, the equivalent family was paying over $10,500.[8] Total mortgage debt has grown from about $6 trillion in 1999 to nearly $13 trillion today.[9]

And let us not forget the increased cost of debt itself. Mortgage lenders have, in recent years, directed a great many home buyers toward subprime loans, which carry higher interest rates and, in many cases, involve balloon payments and other late-breaking surprises. The credit card industry has come up with a bewildering array of similarly unexpected fees and adjustments, which can triple your interest because of a marginally late payment or preemptively raise the interest on one card because you were delinquent in paying another.

Lenders used to base their contracts and business plans on the assumption that people would pay their debts reliably. Since the 1970s (for reasons explored in Chapter 2), the industry has been generating more of its revenues from people's slipups—and constructing deals that make slipups more likely. By the time borrowers get into really deep trouble, debt service itself has often become a big part of the story. In a 2004 bankruptcy case, Capital One analyzed the debts of eighteen North Carolina cardholders; interest and fees, on average, accounted for more than half the money owed.[10]

In the 2007 documentary *Maxed Out*, director James Scurlock presents a grim picture of the American lending industry and the lives of those caught in its clutches. Actually, Scurlock set out to tell a different story—the more familiar one of crazed consumerism and "aspirational" spending. What changed his mind? Exposure to reality. "We're all led to believe that people get into financial trouble because they are irresponsible," Scurlock explained. "But I've learned that most people are getting in trouble because the banks and credit card companies are setting their customers up to fail. . . . Why? The more credit they give us, the more credit we need."[11]

Frugality and consumerism have their place in any discussion of debt, to be sure. Few of us have not made spending choices that we regret. America as a nation might do well to question the sums of private money expended on Botox surgery, SUVs, and designer clothing for children and teens. These luxury markets are booming, though, mainly because a growing number of people at the top of the income scale can afford such things. The debt that should worry us as a society is that borne by tens of millions of middle- and low-income families for whom there is no easy way out, and luxuries have very little to do with it. Americans are borrowing more because incomes have failed to keep up with the cost of health care, housing, and other basic needs. They're borrowing more because, increasingly often, a fraying public safety net has left them to face financial emergencies by themselves. And they're paying a higher price for their borrowing because of the anything-goes attitude of the lending industry.

To understand debt in today's America, we need to expand our perspective beyond individual choice and consumerism and consider a context of private-sector practices, public policy choices, and macroeconomic trends. We need to look around, and we need to look back—at a set of sweeping changes in the forces that shape our buying and borrowing decisions.

GOING BACK ON THE DEAL

From the mid-1940s into the early 1970s, the United States enjoyed a nearly thirty-year run of economic growth. This remarkable surge of prosperity was fueled by pent-up consumer demand and the fact that, of all the rich countries, ours had been touched the least by the devastation of World War II. But there were psychological and social as well as economic forces at work. The Great Depression had taught many well-off Americans to identify with the less fortunate. The war had made us newly conscious of our interdependence and the magnitude of what we could accomplish by working together. Picking up on the emergency agenda of the New Deal, postwar America resolved to share its prosperity more widely and do more to protect people from adversity.

That commitment was expressed in government programs and government investment: the postwar decades were the years of the GI bill (which helped millions of returning soldiers go to college and buy homes with low-interest mortgages), the interstate highway system, and the Higher Education Act of 1965. But the private sector also played its part. In the United States, more than in other developed nations, employers became the primary delivery mechanism for health and pension benefits.

Government encouraged this directly, through tax subsidies, and indirectly, through policies that strengthened the bargaining power of unions. As president, Franklin Roosevelt believed in unions. He also believed in capitalism, and assumed that one was good for the other. With the support of Congress, the Roosevelt administration wrote that conviction into laws that helped organized labor reach its high-water mark. By the end of the war, 40 percent of the private-sector workforce was unionized, and union and nonunion firms alike felt pressure to be competitive on the benefits front as well as the wage front.[12]

What came to be known as the postwar social contract also reflected a softening of the old enmity between labor and management. Companies provided job stability, regular increases in pay, and social insurance protection; workers showed their loyalty by putting in consistent, forty-hour weeks and caring about the quality of the goods and services they produced. Many believed that business as well as labor benefited from this arrangement, and for much of the twentieth century, economic experience seemed to bear this out.[13]

A slowly rising level of good debt was one of the hallmarks of this era. Suburban, tree-lined neighborhoods with cookie-cutter homes accommodated returning soldiers and their families; with federal programs lowering down payment thresholds and lengthening repayment periods, homeownership surged.[14] As the demand for consumer goods grew, installment credit for automobiles, refrigerators, and other big-ticket items increased sharply, from $2.6 billion in 1945 to $103.9 billion in 1970.[15] Even as more Americans went into deeper debt, widespread job stability and a regulated market meant that those debts were generally issued on fair terms and could be paid off in a reasonable span of time.

At the end of the 1960s, increased competition from Europe and Asia, along with the guns-and-butter budgets of the Vietnam War, put the brakes on the postwar boom. Then came the oil-price shock of the mid-1970s. Productivity growth plummeted, inflation shot up, and the economy went into a tailspin.[16] With imports threatening them from one side and corporate raiders from the other, some of the giants of American manufacturing went into downsizing mode. Thousands of middle-class blue-collar workers lost their livelihoods and saw their skills devalued. The jobs they eventually found were, in many cases, not only less well paid but less stable than those they had lost. In this new economic era, Americans would typically change jobs half a dozen times or more in an adult lifetime and companies would pick up and move from one state to another, or clear out of the country, in order to save on labor costs.

The things the postwar social contract had provided—dependable health care, retirement security, help paying for higher education and buying a home—were more important than ever. But the method of providing them needed rethinking. If the leaders of the American auto industry had been able to imagine then what they see now—worker and retiree benefits contributing more to the price of the typical car than steel does—they might have been in the forefront of the fight for national health insurance.[17] If that quest had succeeded, Detroit would be in a more competitive position not only against Japanese and Korean automakers, but against U.S.-owned plants across the border in Canada, where health insurance has long been paid for out of general tax dollars. But in the auto industry and other industries, management tended to focus on short-term fixes like import quotas and relief from environmental rules. Even as corporations were taking steps to reduce the cost of employer benefits, many corporate leaders joined in the chorus of voices opposing efforts to create a viable public alternative. Corporations, through their lobbyists and trade associations and an expanding network of corporate-funded think tanks, took the easy way out, blaming America's economic problems on taxes, regulation, and "big government."

After Ronald Reagan won the presidency in 1980, government-bashing become a government mission. As employers cut back on benefits, the public sector, too, began to walk away from its obligations. Public investment had been crucial to economic opportunity and the expansion of the middle class as far back as the canal- and railroad-building of the 1800s; now it withered. With his decision to fire more than 11,000 striking air traffic controllers, President Reagan made harsh anti-labor tactics widely acceptable to private employers, accelerating organized labor's decline.[18] In the mania for deregulation, laws and rules were revoked or went unenforced. The safety net measures that remained—Social Security, unemployment insurance, the minimum wage—fell far short of providing the security that American workers needed in order to deal with the new challenges facing them.[19]

THE BIG DISCONNECT

For a brief time, the implications of this great pullback were obscured by the high-tech boom and the broader economic resurgence of the late 1990s. Inflation came down and stayed down; productivity soared, and the labor market eventually tightened, boosting incomes and creating a new sense of optimism.[20] The strong economy even produced a brief uptick in employer-sponsored health insurance, while the stock market bubble made employee 401(k) plans look like a satisfactory alternative to the defined-benefit plans they had replaced. When the bubble burst, though, it became apparent that the trends unleashed by the economic dislocations of the 1970s and 1980s were still playing out.

A moment of awakening came late in the 2006 election campaign, when the Bush administration sought to shift public attention away from Iraq and the war on terrorism toward what the president repeatedly called the "strong" economy. The economy *was* strong, according to the usual measures—productivity, output, inflation, even the official rate of unemployment. How, then, to explain why election day exit polls and other surveys revealed high levels of anxiety and pessimism, with half of all voters rating the economy "not good" or "poor," and only 30 percent saying that life would be better for the next generation?[21]

Much of the answer lay in the simple fact that, despite an expanding economy and strong productivity growth, real median income was lower in 2005 than it had been in 2000.[22] The state of "the economy," in other words, no longer bore any necessary relation to most people's economic experience—and Americans had noticed.

The Bush administration hastened to point out that inequality had been rising long before George W. Bush entered the White House. It had not been a front-burner political issue, though, because Americans had been told that they were up against the deep and impersonal forces of globalization. New technology and expanding trade, in other words, had undermined the earning power of those without advanced skills or college degrees, creating a widening "skills gap."

That was a plausible story when experts first started telling it, a quarter century ago. During the 1980s and early 1990s, the "education premium"—the added earning power of a four-year college degree—rose dramatically, while blue-collar workers lagged far behind. Indeed, Americans took the skills gap theory to heart, going to college in record numbers, and going deep into debt to do so.[23] But today's graduates enter an economy in which the big rewards are reserved for a small few. It's a fine time to be a CEO, an investment banker, or a corporate lawyer; meanwhile, computer programmers, teachers, and other professionals face perils similar to those that first rocked the blue-collar world in the late 1970s. Between 2000 and 2005, the earnings of college graduates as a whole fell by about 5 percent on average. "The Americans who should be prospering in a knowledge economy," *Business Week* observed, "are instead taking it on the chin."[24]

Market economies necessarily produce some measure of economic inequality, and most Americans have long accepted that feet. Historically, their acceptence has rested on faith in hard work, education, and ability as the key to getting ahead. In today's America, that faith no longer commands respect. Productivity gains are not being widely shared. Americans are working longer and harder to stay in place, while the gains from the strong economic growth of the past several years have failed to make their way into middle-class paychecks. Over the past two decades, the cost of living has climbed nearly 90 percent, while incomes for the bottom 60 percent of households have risen, on average, only 5 to 15 percent.[25] In our mythology, we remain a land of opportunity. In real life, the United States has become more stratified as well as more unequal. A low-income family's chances of moving up the economic ladder are lower today than they were in the 1970s— and lower in the United States than in many European countries.[26]

The United States remains a fabulously rich society by global and historical standards. Behind the discouraging aggregate numbers, many individual Americans have gained in financial terms, and life has been improved for almost all of us by technological advances—automatic teller machines, computers, and the Internet—that don't show up in the income data.

To understand the high levels of anxiety, however, we need to look at some important statistical omissions on the downside. One is the extraordinary jump in the cost of basic expenses. A typical two-earner family today spends about 80 percent more on housing, 74 percent more on health insurance, and 42 percent more on transportation than did a typical one-earner family in the early 1970s.[27] Many families spend thousands of dollars on child care, a largely nonexistent expense a generation ago. These fixed costs (along with taxes) consumed about half the income of a typical one-earner family in the 1970s; today, a typical two-earner family devotes three-quarters of its income to such costs. Through the groundbreaking work of Elizabeth Warren and Amelia Warren Tyagi, we know that after an average two-income family covers the essentials of home, car, insurance, and child care payments, it has less money left over today than did an average single-income family in the early 1970s; and that's true even with the added hours of labor—and added stress—that result from having two people in the paid workforce.[28]

Americans are working longer, commuting farther, and, as Jacob Hacker argues in his book *The Great Risk Shift*, contending with unprecedented levels of economic turbulence.[29] With the erosion of benefits and a declining savings rate, ordinary families are living closer to the edge—one serious medical problem or professional setback away from disaster. To understand why people are so troubled by the state of the economy, you have to consider all these complicating factors—and one more: rising debt.

AN UNSAFE NET

Despite its deep connection to the drastic economic changes our nation has undergone, debt is widely viewed as a matter of personal responsibility. That's how many financial management counselors, social critics, and champions of the free market depict the problem. And it's how many people view their own debt.

Americans generally don't like to talk about their money—whether it's the money they have or the money they owe. About half the population would refuse to discuss their debts with a friend, according to one recent survey.[30] Give people a chance to speak anonymously, though, and they express strong feelings and tell parallel stories. Many describe a precarious financial existence in which, as one woman in a California focus group put it, "You pray to God that none of your children get sick or that something like the refrigerator doesn't break down."[31]

Surveys conducted in 2005 for Demos and the Center for Responsible Lending unearthed very little of the stereotypical extravagance that is associated with debt. Many people, on the other hand, said that debt had caused them to go without vacations, appliances, and restaurant meals.

Debt-stressed Americans have cut back on frills, in other words, and many have cut back on necessities as well. In one of the surveys, a forty-six-year-old diabetic from Ohio spoke of discontinuing treatment for a shoulder injury "because I couldn't afford it." For the same reason, he said he had begun to stretch out the intervals between visits to a diabetes specialist.[32] Credit card debt is forcing many college students to cut back on their course loads or work long and draining hours to make ends meet. "We lose more students to credit card debt than to academic failure," a University of Indiana administrator commented in 1998.[33]

Debt problems have led some people to postpone—or even abandon—plans to buy a home. "We'd be in a house if it weren't for our credit card debt," another focus-group participant reported. "So it really has stopped us from doing stuff that probably everybody does. But we've never missed a payment. That's our goal—we've never, ever missed one in our lives."[34]

Well over half the households using credit cards for basic living expenses had less than $1,000 in nonretirement savings.[35] Many felt trapped in a pattern of using credit cards in place of funds traditionally set aside for "rainy days."

Against this backdrop of stagnant wages, rising economic volatility, and an eroding safety net, debt has become our de facto safety net: student loan and home mortgage debt helps us get a foothold in the middle class, credit card debt gets us through the rough patches, and predatory lenders swoop in to take advantage of those who hit the hardest times. Health care providers and institutions of higher education have accommodated themselves to the new reality by partnering with banks and other lenders to get people signed up for credit cards and credit lines as part of the intake process. Not knowing any other reality, many young people accept this routinized borrowing as the normal way to get a college degree or medical care.

Debt-as-safety-net, however, is neither safe nor sustainable. It drains money in the form of interest and penalty fees from fragile family finances, aggravating the downside of the turbulent new economy. One late payment can put a family into the penalty zone, which can mean interest payments as high as 30 percent, making the prospects for getting out of debt ever slimmer.

Debt in America wasn't always this way. In fact, at the very time that the economic trends we just described were playing out, the lending industry—newly freed from any meaningful regulation (this will be discussed further in Chapter 2) and armed with increasingly sophisticated technology—was undergoing its own transformation. A key element of this transformation was the development of credit scoring. Credit scores can be riddled with errors—79 percent of them contain mistakes, according to one study; nevertheless they have become the primary mechanism used by lenders to assess risk and to price loans.[36] Relatively small differences in scores can translate into big differences in borrowing costs on credit cards, home loans, and private student loans.

Credit scores have trickled into other areas of our lives, affecting auto insurance premiums and utility bills, and, in some cases, our chances of landing a job. When this sort of risk assessment collides with the use of credit to survive economic cataclysms, those most in need of a safety net all too often find a high-priced loan instead.

GOOD DEBT MEETS BAD DEBT

In our parents' and grandparents' days, there were two kinds of debt: good and bad. Good debt was investment debt; it helped pay for things that would last a lifetime. Good debt was money borrowed from a reputable source at reasonable interest. Bad debt was for discretionary purchases, and the money came from fly-by-night operators who were out to take advantage of you.

Today that distinction has blurred. Good debt is frequently necessary and, at the same time, more risky and expensive. College may not secure upward mobility; now that a bachelor's degree has become a requirement for many middle-class jobs, though, higher education offers some measure of insurance against becoming trapped in the new universe of low-wage dead-end work. But with loans replacing grants as the main form of tuition support, and with need-based aid giving way to merit-based aid, much of it bestowed on people who could manage without the help, many young Americans are forced to take out bigger and bigger loans, which take longer and longer to repay.

The cost of higher education is one large reason why Americans in their twenties now carry an average of about $5,781 in revolving debt above and beyond the nearly $20,000 in student loan debt of the average college graduate.[37] Student loan bills are eating up a larger chunk of young adults' budgets, causing them to turn to credit cards to make up the difference. Meanwhile, higher education costs have played a large role, along with medical debt, in fueling the boom in home mortgage refinance.[38] Altogether, American families extracted some $700 billion in home equity from 2001 to 2005. About half of this borrowing was to pay off higher-cost debt, mostly credit card debt. Between 1973 and 2004, home equity, as a share of total home value in the United States, fell from 68.3 percent to 55 percent. As the housing market cools, many Americans will find themselves owing more than their homes are worth.[39]

Family finances are exposing the fault lines in our nation's economic health, and the lending industry is cashing in. A home mortgage used to be a fairly standardized product—and a safe one. No more. With home prices sky-high in many areas of the country, families turn to interest-only or other types of "exotic" mortgages. Mortgage brokers often exploit the burden of high credit card debt to seduce consumers into the most abusive kinds of mortgages—with devastating long-term consequences. The amount of income that people now dedicate to monthly mortgage debt has reached an all-time high—19 percent in 2006—while the foreclosure rate has more than tripled over the past twenty-five years.[40] By the time the 2007 meltdown in the housing market runs its course, an estimated 2.2 million more homeowners will have been foreclosed on.[41]

So it is getting harder and harder to say where good debt leaves off and bad debt begins. Much of what used to be considered bad debt might now be better described as survival debt—debt used as a safety net to buffer us from economic shocks like job loss or high-priced medical procedures. The explosion of survival debt is like the proverbial canary in the mineshaft; it tells us just how hard today's middle- and low-income families must struggle to stay financially afloat. Student loan debt, mortgage debt, medical debt, credit card debt—they're all profoundly influenced by the economic, social, and political environment. As levels of household debt hit new highs, policymakers should take note. Debt is a personal issue and a family issue. It has become a crucial national issue as well.

2

AN INDUSTRY RUN AMOK

- To help pay a relative's medical bills, Janet Ruiz of Har-risonburg, Virginia, took out a $2,950 auto title loan in February 2005. Unable to keep up with the payments, she found herself owing $16,000 (more than five times the original amount) by April 2006.[1]

- Jeffrey Williams chose a field of study—English—known for generating a surplus of PhDs and a scarcity of well-paid jobs. Seventeen years later, Williams is a tenured professor at Carnegie Mellon University and, despite his good fortune, still paying off his student loans. Every month, he sends in a check for $650; some of the money goes to his own graduate-school debt and some to paying off PLUS loans for his daughter's college. The combined balance stands at $18,465. His daughter has another $16,709 of student-loan debt in her own right.[2]

- To pay off a $1,500 credit card bill and finance some reno-vation, Carol Mackey took out a refinancing loan on her condominium in Rochester Hills, Michigan. The loan produced $18,645 in cash while costing Mackey more than $8,000 in fees. In the process, she traded a $74,000 mortgage with a 7.5 percent annual interest rate for a $100,750 mortgage with a 12.8 percent interest rate. Her monthly payments more than doubled from $510 to $1,103.[3]*

In today's America, overwhelming debt is an everyday condition. That's partly because of pay and benefit trends and public policies that have pushed millions of families toward the financial edge. But it's also because the lending industry has made it harder and harder for people to get out of debt once they fall in. And here is a case where, unfortunately, the truth is well served by a broad-brush generalization. Just as the perils of debt are no longer confined to a few irresponsible borrowers, they are no longer confined to a few irresponsible lenders either. In the age of deregulation, the giants of American lending have taken up the kind of slippery practices that ought to be—that, for the most part, used to be—limited to an irresponsible few.

From a regulation standpoint, there are two kinds of lending institutions: banks and the rest. Banks (including credit unions and the few remaining savings and loans—the few survivors of a period when their name became inseparable from the word "scandal") are a class apart because, in addition to making loans, they

---

* The stories told in this book are those of real people. In some cases, they were interviewed by the authors. In others, we drew the information from newspaper or magazine articles or from online publications, as noted in the text and notes. To protect their anonymity, some people chose to be identified by a pseudonym or a first name only. Where a story had been previously told in another publication, we use the name as it originally appeared.

hold deposits. Through their lending and investing decisions, they can jeopardize the safety of the money that people put in the bank. Their actions can also compromise the integrity of the Federal Reserve and the national system of credit and financial exchange that banks have access to.

Banks can fail and depositors can panic, creating the potential for a chain reaction of failure. More than nine thousand banks (nearly 40 percent of the nation's commercial banks at the time) were forced to shut down, at least briefly, between 1929 and 1933. One that closed forever was the Bank of the United States, among the nation's largest.[4] The bank failures of the Great Depression cost account holders almost $400 million and shook public confidence in the American banking system. The Roosevelt administration responded by creating deposit insurance (provided by the Federal Deposit Insurance Corporation, or FDIC) and by placing stricter limits on the ratio of loans to assets, among other reforms.[5]

DON'T FENCE US IN

But by the 1970s, the Depression was long forgotten and banks were chafing at the many restrictions placed on them. Most banks operated under state rather than federal charters—a tradition dating back to the country's early years, when Americans were deeply suspicious of national power and national banks. Even the minority of banks with federal charters could not do business in more than one state. The number of branches that a bank could have within a state was also regulated, along with the range of products and services that a bank could offer. Savings accounts were permitted, for example, while higher-interest money market accounts were not.[6]

In the lending industry, as in air travel and telephone service, the champions of deregulation had a simple story to tell. It was about breaking down walls, eliminating burdensome rules and procedures, and stimulating competition for the consumer's sake. But banks had an industry-specific case to make as well. In an age of computers and global trade, Americans needed the freedom to cross state lines without being cut off from their money. Bankers and lenders could reasonably say that they, too, needed more freedom, for competitiveness's sake.[7]

One result of regulation had been to make American banks far smaller than those of other countries. In 1985 the United States had fifteen thousand banks—no other Western nation had even one-tenth that many. (Canada, for example, had seventy-one.)[8] How could such a fragmented industry hope to do business on a global playing field? Competitiveness was a potent buzzword in Washington during the 1980s and 1990s. It gave bankers a powerful rationale for what many of them badly wanted: the ability to expand and diversify.

By the late 1970s, they had another argument going for them. State usury laws limited the interest that banks could collect from borrowers; in Arkansas and Texas, for example, the maximum was 10 percent.[9] In the double-digit inflation of the late 1970s and early 1980s, it became just about impossible for banks to make money by lending money. The industry was getting squeezed on the depositor side as well. The Federal Reserve had laid down a rule (known as Regulation Q) that effectively prevented banks from paying more than 5.25 percent interest on deposit accounts. Under the same regulation, checking accounts could not pay any interest at all.[10] Those limits, dating back to the bank failures of Depression times, had been intended to keep bigger banks from driving smaller ones out of business; now they had become a problem for all banks.[11] As the prime rate climbed toward its 1981 peak of 21.5 percent, money flooded out of the nation's banks into mutual funds and money market accounts at rival institutions such as American Express and Merrill Lynch.[12]

So, in their quest for looser regulation, bankers and lenders could make persuasive points; they could also wield a great deal of political clout. Deregulation, to its intellectual purists, meant the removal of subsidies and supports as well as rules and regulations. But that was not what the banking industry and its political allies wanted—and it is certainly not what occurred. One of the first big bank deregulation measures passed by Congress, the Depository Institutions Deregulation and Monetary Control Act of 1980, gave commercial banks, savings banks, and savings and loans the power to offer a variety of new services, including interest-bearing checking accounts (known as NOW accounts). But the same legislation also increased the per-account limit on federal deposit insurance from $40,000 to $100,000.[13]

In the name of deregulation, bankers and lenders were getting increased latitude coupled with increased protection. That combination was an invitation to recklessness. A great many banks responded by venturing into fields they knew little about and making lending decisions based more on market hype or cronyism than on a careful examination of the risks. All this led to the results loosely known as the savings and loan scandal, and a federal bailout costing more than $125 billion in public funds.[14]

SOUTH DAKOTA, HERE WE COME

Bankers and lenders could speak with great indignation about the burdens of complying with different rules in different places and the need for federal "preemption" of state authority. But they were also quite ready to invoke state authority when it suited them. In 1978, the First National Bank of Omaha convinced the Supreme Court that it should be allowed to follow the laws of Nebraska, which had an 18 percent interest cap, in its dealings with credit card holders in Minnesota, which had a 12 percent cap. (A Minnesota bank, Marquette National, had objected.)[15]

Looking on from New York City, Citibank's Walter Wriston saw the possibilities immediately. A national bank could now simply charter itself in a state with lax rules and "export" those rules to the other forty-nine states. (As banks proceeded to do just that, regulatory disputes took on an interstate dimension, creating another argument for the federal government to settle things.) Citibank had tried, and failed, to get New York State to raise its own 12 percent interest limit to "some reasonable amount," as Wriston put it later. Now, thanks to the *Marquette* decision, Wriston realized that he had only to convince another state—any state, however small—to remove all interest limits. Then Citibank could move its credit card operations there and charge whatever interest it saw fit.

The South Dakota legislature soon obliged, and promptly issued an official invitation (as required by federal banking law) to

Citibank to enter the state. "Citibank actually drafted the legislation," former South Dakota governor Bill Janklow recalled. "Literally, we introduced it, and it passed our legislature in one day."[16] Because South Dakota no longer had an interest cap, Citi Card customers across the country could be charged any interest rate. Thus, with little public input or awareness, the concept of usury—rooted in thousands of years of Christian, Jewish, and Muslim tradition—effectively passed out of American law.[17]

In the world of banking and lending, deregulation was a long and complicated affair, in which important decisions often got made with little or no public scrutiny. (See Table 2-1, "Mileposts on the Road to Deregulated Lending.") The industry took full advantage of this disconnected process to achieve results far different from what the theorists had forecast—results that, in many cases, no one with the public interest in mind could possibly have wanted. To appreciate the magnitude of the gulf between theory and practice, consider what happened under the heading of four of deregulation's grand promises: competition, innovation, savings, and fairness.

TABLE 2-1

MILEPOSTS ON THE ROAD TO DEREGULATED LENDING

| 1978 | *Marquette Nat. Bank v. First of Omaha Corp.* | The Supreme Court, citing a obscure 1863 law, rules that for interest rate purposes, bank need pay attention only to their home states, not the states where their borrowers live. South Dakota and Delaware proceed to remove all limits, quickly becoming |

(continued)

TABLE 2-1

MILEPOSTS ON THE ROAD TO DEREGULATED LENDING

(continued)

		the nominal home states of a big part of the American credit card industry
1980	Depository Institutions Deregulation and Monetary Control Act (DIDMCA)	In the name of helping the nation's imperiled banks compete against mutual funds and other upstarts, Congress phases out the deposit interest cap, deregulates interest on first mortgages, and authorizes banks and S&Ls to offer interest-bearing checking accounts known as NOW accounts. Federal deposit insurance jumps from $40,000 to $100,000.
1982	Garn–St. German Depository Institutions Act	Gives broader lending powers to federally chartered savings and loans.
1982	Alternative Mortgage Transaction Parity Act (AMPTA)	Preempts state-level efforts to limit prepayment penalties and late fees on alternative mortgages.
1987	Competitive Equality in Banking Act (CEBA)	Curtails the rise of "nonbank banks."
1994	Riegle-Neal Interstate Banking and Branching Efficiency Act	Removes geographical barriers. A North Carolina bank, for example, can now open a branch in New York, as long as it abides by New York law.
1996	*Smiley v. Citibank*	The Supreme Court decides that credit card fees, like interest, can be limited only by the issuer's home state (which

by now generally means South Dakota or Delaware). New fees proliferate.

1997	Riegle-Neal merger amendment	Congress allows interstate bank mergers. The following year produces the combined Citicorp-Travelers, Bank of America–National Bank, Banc One–First Chicago, and Norwest–Wells Fargo.
1999	Gramm-Leach-Bliley Financial Modernization Act	In the name of global competitiveness, vast new powers are granted to financial holding companies (FHCs). This opens the door to one-stop shopping for financial markets.
2005	Bankruptcy Abuse Prevention and Consumer Protection Act	Responding to credit card companies' complaints of "bankruptcy abuse" and "surprise bankruptcies," Congress erects a series of new hurdles along the path to Chapter 7 protection—the most comprehensive. Some borrowers are required to continue making loan payments even after they go bankrupt.

GRAND PROMISE 1: COMPETITION

Look around your neighborhood, and if you're old enough to remember the days of regulated banks (or the old Christmas tearjerker *It's a Wonderful Life*), you might be inclined to say that deregulation has delivered on this promise. Thirty years ago, if you needed a mortgage or a small-business loan, you were lucky to have more than one or two places to go. Deregulation has brought more players into the act while giving individual lenders the right to offer a wider variety of services. You can see the results in towns and cities across the land. In Sarasota, Florida, for example, some four dozen commercial banks and savings associations stand ready to take your deposit money or loan application. Ten credit unions and an array of payday lenders and subprime mortgage shops add to the options.[18]

Competition has grown by leaps and bounds—in other words, if you define it simply in terms of the number of companies operating in a single local market, which is how industry leaders say it should be defined. To the individual consumer or community, they argue, it shouldn't really matter that with all the mergers and acquisitions of recent years (600 bank mergers in 1997 alone), the number of banks in the country as a whole has been cut in half—from more than 15,000 in 1984 to about 7,500 today.[19]

But lending, in many of its forms, is no longer a local business: certainly not in the realm of credit cards, where the top six companies now handle some 61 percent of all the nation's accounts.[20] Consolidation also matters if you consider the kinds of banks that have been disappearing, and the kinds that have been replacing them. In the ideal of competition described by the champions of deregulation, the differences among banks would be more than skin-deep. Imagine that your loan application had been turned down by a brand-name bank—one of the "large megabanks" characterized by relatively "standardized wares and impersonal service," in the words of J. Alfred Broaddus Jr., a former president of the Federal Reserve Bank of Richmond, Virginia. Your next step, in his optimistic scenario, would be to try your luck with a "high-touch" community bank.[21]

Unfortunately, these smaller institutions, where personal rela-

tionships counted, have been going out of business in droves—
acquired or pushed out by their inability to compete with the
megabanks. That has been especially true in metropolitan markets, and above all in poor communities.[22] By 2004, nearly 44
percent of the full-service banks in Chicago were located in upper-
income zip codes. Chicago's low-income zip codes, on the other
hand, had only 2.3 percent of all full-service branches. In Chicago
and elsewhere, banks have closed inner-city branches and moved to
neighborhoods where they expect to generate bigger profits.[23]

Defenders of deregulation make much of a new crop of independent "novo banks" that are said to be filling the gap. But while
these institutions often portray themselves as neighborhood
banks, most are larger in size and coverage area than the community banks of yesteryear. Like other banks, novo banks often tailor
their services to relatively well-off customers, with minimum-
balance requirements and overdraft and bounced-check fees that
make these institutions unfriendly to much of the population.
Some of the novo banks themselves have joined in the industry's
flight away from low- and moderate-income neighborhoods.[24]
That flight has had a profound effect on the availability of loans
for minority-owned small businesses. It helps explain a startling
150 percent decline in the number of interest-bearing accounts
held by low-income Americans.[25]

GRAND PROMISE 2: INNOVATION

In the old days, banking was a stodgy business, no doubt about it.
One bank's services were much like another's. If your loan application got turned down by National Mutual, you could pretty

much count on getting the same result at Mutual National across the street.

Deregulation, it was assumed, would ignite the fires of innovation and bring forth all manner of new products and services. And so it has. Who can deny the ingenuity of the zero percent introductory interest rate? Or the balloon payment? Like these examples, though, many of the industry's other recent innovations have been designed for one of two purposes—either to lure customers in or to saddle them with unanticipated costs. It is ideas of *that* kind, not ones that might save people money or make their options clearer, that seem to have spread furthest and fastest. In the mid-1990s, as interest rates went down, a few credit card companies began imposing penalty interest rates for late payments; now almost all do. Many charge between 22 and 29 percent for up to a year following the first infraction—a huge increase from the 1990s, when late fees averaged around $9.[26] According to a 2000 survey by the Public Interest Research Group (PIRG), 69 percent of credit card issuers customarily raised a cardholder's rate after one late payment, up from 46 percent in 1998.[27]

The fee frenzy was set off by another industry-friendly Supreme Court decision—an ill-considered afterthought to the *Marquette* ruling, in which the Court had taken away the authority of the states to protect their citizens against usury. In *Smiley v. Citibank*—a 1996 case—the Court ruled that there was no real difference between interest charges and other loan fees; and so, banks were now free to export one state's loose rules concerning fees as well as interest. Once again, credit card companies were quick to capitalize. Total consumer penalty fees jumped from $1.7 billion in 1996 to $17.1 billion in 2006. Such fees, which now average $34, have become the industry's fastest-growing revenue source.[28] One of the nation's largest card issuers, MBNA—now part of Bank of America—imposes a $35 fee on all delinquent cardholders with balances over $1,001.[29] To bring in even more revenue, most major issuers have reduced the late-payment grace period from fourteen days to no days.[30]

The zero percent teaser rate is one of several marketing innovations credited to Andrew Kahr, one of the founders of Providian Financial Services, which pioneered the subprime credit card market in the late 1990s. At Kahr's urging, Providian cut the required monthly payment from 5 percent to 2 percent of a cardholder's balance, although a 2 percent payment would in many cases not even cover the interest. The result was higher profits for credit card companies—and deeper financial trouble for customers.

After a bogus "credit protection" plan attracted the notice of state and federal regulators, Providian agreed in 2000 to a $300 million settlement with consumers.[31] By that time, Kahr had moved on, and so had a number of his ideas, which were well on the way to becoming standard practice throughout the industry. Kahr's methods rested, in the view of industry critics, on an "optimism bias" that leads many borrowers to focus on the most immediate and obvious costs of a loan, ignoring charges that they do not expect to incur. (The fee craze has, incidentally, made it all but impossible to compare one card's total costs with another.)

Industry leaders insist that they have no desire to mislead or confuse. They have been anything but shy, however, in their opposition to rules that would ensure greater clarity. In 2001, California enacted a law requiring credit card statements to carry a prominent notice informing customers how much it would cost them, and how long it would take, to pay off their balances at the minimum-payment rate. Supporters of the proposal pointed out that many people were paying the minimum without realizing that they were likely to remain in debt for decades that way. (With a $5,000 balance on a card that carried a 17 percent interest rate, the 2 percent minimum payment set by many card companies would mean forty years of payments, ultimately adding up to more than $16,000.) Such disclosures had long been routine with fixed-term auto loans and home mortgages. Nevertheless, the American Bankers Association filed suit to block the legislation.[32] Although the industry seemed to have no trouble keeping up with the complexities of its own rules, it depicted the California proposal as a costly burden. A federal judge in Sacramento agreed.[33]

GRAND PROMISE 3: SAVINGS

When an industry of independent, locally based companies is taken over by national chains, prices plummet. Think Wal-Mart. Think McDonald's. On that assumption, just about everyone involved in the early deregulation debates agreed that big banks would be more efficient than small ones, with some of the savings passed on to their customers.

Yet study after study has failed to find these benefits. In fact, by most of the obvious measures, costs are higher, not lower. Credit card rates, after shooting up to 15 and 20 percent during the era of hyperinflation, have remained mysteriously "sticky" ever since. During the year 2001, the Federal Reserve lowered interest rates eleven times, from a starting point of 6.24 percent all the way down to 3.88 percent.[34] Credit card interest rates, meanwhile, fell only marginally, from 15.71 percent to 14.89 percent.[35] The net effect has been a substantial widening in the "spread" between the interest banks pay the Fed and the interest that credit card borrowers pay the banks.

While bank executives maintain that their interest rates are justified by the costs and risks of the credit card business, the industry has been on a profit-making tear for nearly two decades. In 1990, reported pretax profits came to $6.4 billion; by 2005, they had reached $30.6 billion—an increase of nearly 400 percent. This combination of record profits and widening spread is the kind of pattern often seen when a small number of corporate players achieve a dominant position in their field and enter into tacit (or not so tacit) arrangements to keep prices high. And that is, of course, another danger of the kind of consolidation that has occurred in the banking industry, where the assets of the 10 biggest companies now exceed those of the next biggest 150 companies.[36]

But while the dynamics of oligopoly pricing seem to have been operating in the so-called retail end of the lending industry, the forces of competition have evidently functioned well in the so-called wholesale end. Thus, one set of customers—corporations and affluent individuals—has gained, while another set—low- and middle-income borrowers—has lost. One way to put the contrast in focus is by comparing the annual interest rates charged to corporate customers and to individual credit card holders. In 2006, the industry-wide average for corporate loans was 3.8 percent; for credit cards, it was 13.21 percent—three and a half times greater.[37]

Interest rates are not the only place where banks seem to adopt very different practices with these two classes of borrowers. On the retail end, they assert the right to change the terms of a credit card contract "at any time for any reason," as JPMorgan Chase forthrightly announces on one of its Visa card terms sheets. You won't find such clauses in the world of commercial loans. Bankers seem to think their corporate customers wouldn't stand for it.

GRAND PROMISE 4: JUSTICE

In pre-deregulation days, the opinions or prejudices of a few "old boys" often controlled the fortunes of a great many would-be borrowers.[38] For women, African Americans, and Latinos, among others, applying for credit could be an uphill struggle. Entire neighborhoods were redlined—that is, declared off limits.

Deregulation was promoted as a way to bring about a badly needed "democratization of credit," in the oft-quoted words of Lawrence Lindsey, an economic policy adviser to the first President Bush.[39] But on the democratization front, too, the results have been mixed at best. Minority homeownership has increased, along with minority access to credit cards and other lending instruments. As low-income Americans and people of color have gained the ability to borrow, however, many have been channeled into a world of manipulative practices and fringe players. Low-income customers and people of color are much more likely to be paying interest rates of 20 percent or more on their credit cards. Deregulation has led a great many banks to close inner-city branches and focus their energies elsewhere. More choice for the banking industry, in other words, has meant less choice for many consumers.[40]

As banks have departed, payday loan shops, check-cashing joints, and other second-tier or fringe lenders have arrived. Using the poor as laboratory subjects, the subprime mortgage industry developed a set of practices linked (even before the meltdown of early 2007) to alarmingly high default rates; some 20 percent of the subprime refinancing loans issued between 1998 and 2002 ended in foreclosure, compared with 1.1 percent of traditional mortgage loans. African Americans and Latinos, who together make up 27 percent of the population, have consistently accounted for over 80 percent of the subprime customer base; economic factors barely begin to explain this enormous disproportion. In Chicago, one study found that upper-income African Americans were nearly four times more likely than comparable white borrowers to get a subprime loan, while upper-income Hispanics were more than twice as likely.[41]

In theory, the big banks would respond to the new predatory practices by offering better products to the same customers. Instead of competing with the fringe players, however, major lenders have often chosen to make deals with them. When the *Marquette* decision came down in 1978, it applied to banks alone. Sensing an opportunity for profit, however, some banks began "renting" their *Marquette* rights to payday loan companies, providing them with a loophole around state laws. Other banks went further. In 2005, Citibank acquired First Capital Associates, a subprime mortgage company that had been disciplined repeatedly for questionable lending practices. HSBC, another giant, joined forces with H&R Block—long associated with high-interest tax-refund loans. Capital One is one of a number of major companies that have copied the fringe lenders by bringing out a subprime credit card—its EZN card, which charges $88 in fees for a $112 line of credit.[42]

KEYSTONE CREDIT COPS

Thirty years into the story of deregulation, the gulf between promises and results has widened into a chasm. Proponents, it would be charitable to say, failed to anticipate the potential for oligopoly pricing in this tightly networked industry. They evidently gave little thought to the phenomenon of "information asymmetry" between knowledgeable corporate sellers and naïve individual buyers. And they seem to have left another peril out of their calculations entirely: the effects of concentrated political power.

In 1992, an estimated 20 percent of all the political action committee (PAC) money flowing to our elected representatives in Washington came from the financial services industry. In 1993 and 1994—the period leading up to passage of the Riegle-Neal Act, which smoothed the way for interstate banking—the industry gave more than $100 million to House and Senate candidates, dividing its largesse almost equally between the two major parties.[43] A decade later, the banks turned on the spigots again, putting a comparably huge sum of money into the quest for a bankruptcy "reform" law that scarcely anyone outside the banking industry had sought.[44]

Big banks today have little to fear from the agencies supposedly responsible for holding them to the terms of the law. Some public officials might be described as asleep at the switch; others have been remarkably alert in championing the interests of those they seem to perceive as their constituents—the banks themselves.

This is an old problem, and there's a name for it: captive regulation. It has been aggravated, in the banking industry's case, by an unusual "choose your own regulator" setup. A credit card issuer can opt for either a state or a federal charter; if it makes the first choice, oversight responsibility falls to the Federal Reserve or the Federal Deposit Insurance Corporation (FDIC). If it decides on a national charter, it gets supervised by the Office of the Comptroller of the Currency (OCC). The OCC, remarkably, receives its funding from the very companies it regulates, in the form of fees to have their applications processed and businesses examined.[45]

When it comes to lending-industry abuses, state officials and agencies have been much more active—and more effective—than their federal counterparts. A number of attorney generals have tried to crack down on abusive credit card practices in recent years. The results might have been more impressive, though, if the OCC had not come to the credit card companies' assistance in case after case by arguing that it alone had jurisdiction.[46] When the Supreme Court, in *Smiley,* decided that fees were actually "interest by another name," it took that position at OCC's urging.[47]

And yet the "deregulated" lending industry continues to enjoy vast public subsidies in the form of deposit insurance (and other depositor-protection policies) as well as low-cost credit through the Federal Reserve and access to the federally supported national payments system.[48]

These benefits used to come with obligations attached. The Community Reinvestment Act of 1979 was a notable attempt to maintain a sense of mutual accountability in an age of deregulation. It required banking institutions to provide services to disadvantaged groups in their local communities. Many banks responded by moving away from the communities that the CRA rules had been intended to help. Adding insult to injury, some banks formed financial alliances with the check-cashing outlets and payday loan shops that were the most conspicuous credit options left in some of those communities. JPMorgan Chase and Wells Fargo, for example, are part of a network of banks extending credit to ACE Cash Express, a nationwide chain whose menu of high-priced services includes money orders, bill payment, money wiring, and payday loans where state law permits.[49]

What many in the lending industry hoped to accomplish through deregulation was freedom from public accountability and continued public support. To a great extent, that is what the industry has gotten. Consumers, meanwhile, have largely been left to fend for themselves.

3

GOTCHA!

Take an inventory of your wallet. If you find a few credit cards in there—or even a few more than a few—you can count yourself an average American of the early twenty-first century.[1] A credit card almost qualifies as a necessity nowadays. Try renting a car, booking an airplane trip, or engaging in almost any kind of online commerce without one.

In fact, convenience rather than credit is what many people are after when they apply for that first card. But circumstances change, and if you are like the majority of Americans, you have looked at your credit card statement in horror on at least a few occasions. Between 1989 and 2006, the nation's total credit card charges increased from about $69 billion a year to more than $1.8 trillion.[2] The proportion of households carrying a balance from month to month has grown (it was 58 percent in 2004), and the average amount owed by those households has increased by a staggering 88 percent—from $2,768 in 1989 to $5,219 in 2004.[3]

In 2005, Demos and the Center for Responsible Lending commissioned a survey of more than 1,100 middle- and low-income families with a recent history of unpaid balances. Nearly half the households in that survey reported having at least $5,000 in credit card debt; one-third owed $10,000 or more.[4]

A small fraction of these people traced their indebtedness back to spending on items that were neither critical nor necessary, such as a kitchen remodeling or the purchase of a major appliance. Far more pointed to basic living expenses such as rent and groceries, a medical or dental emergency, or a car repair. Many had started using credit cards in this way after a job loss. The survey results suggested a pattern in which one big blow—or one big burden— leaves resources so depleted that a family has to borrow for unusual and ordinary needs alike.

So let's say you owe a few thousand dollars or more. That, too, you may rest assured, is perfectly normal; and unless you are a very unusual borrower, you didn't run up your balance buying Manolo Blahnik shoes or Patek Philippe wristwatches. More likely, you slipped into debt while dealing with one of life's little financial emergencies. Then you found yourself using credit cards to cover ordinary living expenses—gas, groceries, utilities, rent— because it was the only way you knew how.[5]

A TOUGH SELL

Consumer credit is an old idea. Credit cards are a fairly new one. The Eureka! moment came, according to industry legend, one night in 1949 at Major's Cabin Grill, a restaurant near the Empire State Building in New York City. A finance company executive named Frank X. McNamara had invited two associates to dine with him. At meal's end, McNamara realized he had forgotten his wallet, and he was forced to call his wife, who came around with the money. A businessperson should not have to be so cash dependent, he decided. A year later, McNamara was back at the same restaurant paying his bill with a card (made of paper, not yet plastic) that identified him as one of the charter members of the Diners Club. He was also its founder and first chief executive.[6]

Department stores had been giving out charge cards as far back as the 1920s. A few of the major oil and gas companies had adopted the practice in the prewar years, allowing motorists to fill up their tanks when they had outrun their cash-supply lines. (Well before that, in 1887, Edward Bellamy's utopian novel *Looking Backward* imagined a world in which cards replaced cash entirely.)[7] But the pre–Diners Club cards were intended to cultivate loyalty to a single company. McNamara was the first to conceive of card-issuing as a business unto itself, and his was the first card that multiple merchants would accept. He started out with fourteen restaurants, generating his revenue from a 7 percent commission on every purchase. Within three years, the Diners Club had one hundred thousand members.[8]

The Diners Club required full payment at the end of the month.[9] The idea was to make life easier for traveling salespeople and others who, in a cardless world, had to carry dangerously large sums of cash or search for businesses that would take their checks. The original American Express card, which appeared in 1958, followed the same pay-up-or-else policy—it was a charge card, not a credit card. That same year, Bank of America introduced its BankAmericard (later renamed Visa), which allowed people to repay over time. Soon it was issuing Visa cards on behalf of other banks, in return for a licensing fee.

Bank of America was a California institution.[10] So were all the early Visa card licensees; and so were the banks that in 1966 formed a rival group known originally as the Interbank Card Association and later as MasterCard.[11] In casual borrowing, as in casual dress, it was West Coast executives who led the way. Back East, many bankers worried about what they saw as a dangerous loosening of lending standards. Shortly before Christmas of 1966, their fears were confirmed when a group of midwestern banks sent out roughly 5 million unsolicited credit cards; the addressees turned out to include an unfortunate number of convicted felons, toddlers, and dogs. The experiment set off a tidal wave of fraud and losses, with crooked postal workers allegedly passing cards to organized-crime figures and suburban couples being billed thousands of dollars for cards they had never seen.[12]

The industry was still trying to find its balance when it got hit by the runaway inflation of the late 1970s and early 1980s. New York State had a usury law with a 12 percent limit on the interest that banks could charge borrowers. When "you are lending money at 12 percent and paying 20 percent," Citibank's Walter Wriston said later, "you don't have to be Einstein to realize you're out of business."[13] By 1980, Citibank had lost more than $1 billion on its credit card operations. Some of the other big players weren't doing much better.[14]

After the Supreme Court came to the rescue with the *Marquette* decision in 1978 (giving banks in high-interest states the right to "export" loans to customers in other states), Citibank moved its card-issuing unit to South Dakota, while Chase, Manufacturers Hanover, and others set up shop in Delaware. Once usury had been effectively legalized, the card companies made a startling discovery: not only could they get away with charging stratospheric interest when inflation was out of control; it turned out they could get away with it at other times, too. That realization transformed the credit card business from a money loser into a money gusher. Between 1980 and 1990, the number of credit cards doubled, credit card spending increased more than fivefold, and the balance owed by the average card-holding American family jumped from $518 to nearly $2,700.[15]

SITTING STILL FOR THE SQUEEZE

In the spring of 1990, three words sent convulsions through the credit card world. Those words—emblazoned across ads for a new AT&T credit card—were "No Annual Fee." AT&T's offer generated more than a quarter of a million responses on the first day, prompting other companies to bring out no-fee cards of their own.[16] Soon the $20 annual fees of the 1980s were history.[17] Eventually they would seem fairly benign, compared to what replaced them.

The modern credit card is really two products in one: a borrowing tool and a payment tool. With the disappearance of the annual fee, the cost burden shifted squarely onto the backs of the so-called revolvers—or serious borrowers—giving "convenience users," who routinely paid their bills in full, a free ride.[18] Unsurprisingly, one bank after another soon found that it had too few revolvers and too many convenience users (or, as some in the industry began calling them, "deadbeats"). To right the balance, lenders were tempted to go after people with shakier finances, since they were more likely to borrow; the only difficulty was that they would presumably also be more likely to default. Higher risk would mean higher interest rates at a time when they were already sky-high. In 1992, the industry average was 17.8 percent, about the same as it had been in 1980, even though the prime rate had meanwhile plunged from 13.4 to 3.5 percent. (In 2007, the average rate was 13.79 percent.)[19] The industry had already taken flak from consumer groups and elected officials for the widening spread between its own borrowing costs and those of its customers. Only a last-minute warning from the White House had kept Congress, in 1991, from passing a national usury law proposed by New York Republican senator Alfonse D' Amato.[20] Most lenders figured they were already charging as much as the market would bear.

But most lenders were not as imaginative as a group of upstarts in San Francisco. Providian, as their company became known after a 1994 merger, had been founded (with backing from the Parker Pen Company) by Andrew Kahr. The company was shaped by Kahr's belief that the industry had focused on the wrong customer base—that is, on middle- and upper-middle-class people who would presumably make large purchases and be unlikely to default. Providian took a very different approach, going after customers that most credit card issuers wanted no part of. Divorced women, housewives who had never owned much of anything, people with sketchy or suspect credit records—Kahr and his colleagues believed there was gold in those unmined hills: vast numbers of customers who would eventually pay their debts, but who needed credit so badly that they would not look too closely at what it cost them.[21]

Kahr, who had earned a doctorate from MIT at the age of twenty (with a thesis entitled "A Minimal Reduction Class for the *Entschei-*

dungsproblem"), devised a set of supercomplicated formulas and scoring systems to identify his new universe of customers. Then he began working on ways to increase revenue without being too obvious about it. Demonstrating a flair for English as well as math, he pointed out that a Buyers Club program offering 1 percent rebates could be promoted as a "discount on everything you buy," or, by throwing in an occasional higher rebate, as a discount of "up to 30 percent." When others in the company wanted to do away with the customary monthlong grace period, Kahr proposed a "limited grace period" instead—one so constructed that, he explained, "almost no one gets the benefit of it."[22]

Kahr believed in choosing the right words—and putting them in the right place. Often that meant a place where customers were unlikely to notice. In lieu of an annual fee, some of Providian's cards came with an "automatic credit protection" plan that cost far more than any annual fee, although, as some customers had the misfortune to discover, it provided very little protection. If the company had charged a flat sum for this dubious service—say, $7.95 a month—it would have to have appeared in a disclosure box known as the Schumer box, after Senator Charles Schumer of New York, who sponsored the legislation requiring it. Kahr therefore suggested a variable fee pegged to the size of the credit line; that way, it could be relegated to the fine print. "Excellent suggestion," Providian's CEO, Shailesh Mehta, wrote in the margins of Kahr's memo.[23]

Kahr was no longer an employee when he set down these thoughts. Concluding that day-to-day management was not his forte, he had given up the CEO's job and moved to the south of France, where he continued to advise the company on a consulting basis.[24] His memos to Mehta and others became evidence in a tangle of class-action lawsuits and federal and local investigations, which ended with Providian agreeing to pay more than $400 million to cardholders and their attorneys. By that time, Kahr's consulting deal had ended and the company was led by a new management team—one that, according to a Providian spokesperson, would "totally reject and would never tolerate the attitudes those memos display."[25] Other lending-industry executives also went to some lengths to dissociate themselves from Kahr's attitudes. His practices, however, were another matter.

Providian had been a pioneer in the marketing of so-called subprime credit cards. In the lending world, the word "prime" takes its meaning from the prime rate, which is the rate of interest charged by banks to the borrowers they consider most reliable. The prime sector of any lending market consists of the safest borrowers and situations; subprime means everything and everybody else. Since Kahr and his colleagues showed the way, subprime credit cards have become a huge industry.

Today, major banks as well as fringe players are involved, sometimes jointly. HSBC, the world's third-largest bank, owns Orchard Bank, a subprime company; it also has a refund anticipation loan (RAL) deal with H&R Block, the largest tax preparation company in the United States. Their RAL program provides taxpayers with short-term, fee-laden, triple-digit-interest loans that are secured by prospective tax refunds.[26] Capital One purveys the subprime EZN card in addition to its mainstream cards; some customers apply to Capital One expecting a normal card with a moderate interest rate, but wind up with a subprime card instead.[27]

Before making headlines as the target of lawsuits and investigations, Providian gained the industry's attention with its financial performance. During the mid-1990s, the company enjoyed an average account balance of $4,500, while the industry norm was $1,800. It had a pretax profit margin of 5 percent, compared with an average of 3.2 percent, and its profits had grown by 20 percent a year or more for a decade.[28] It had achieved these results by, among other things, using low "introductory" interest rates to draw in customers; turning its credit limit into a revenue stream by approving "over the limit" purchases and charging extra for them; and lowering the minimum monthly payment to 2 percent of the balance—a level that could take up to half a century to pay off. All these techniques went on to become standard practice, not just in the subprime end of the market but across the spectrum of credit card issuers. (The only one that the industry has abandoned is the 2 percent minimum payment—and not by choice: in December 2005, federal bank regulators issued new rules that effectively raised the minimum payment to 4 percent.)[29]

In the early days of the credit card business, the cost of borrowing consisted largely of interest and the rate was clearly stated. In the new world that Kahr and his colleagues helped define, the official interest rate became just one among many charges, and not necessarily the most important one. (See "Land of the Fee" on p. 46.)

The Supreme Court also deserves a share of the credit, though. Before the *Smiley* decision on credit card fees, the typical credit card late fee was about $13. By 2005, it was nearly $34.[30] All told, late fees and over-the-limit fees generated $14.8 billion in revenue for the card companies in 2005.[31] Under the terms of many credit card contracts, late payments now also trigger a "penalty" or "default" interest rate; the average was 27 percent in 2005, with many

LAND OF THE FEE

An Incomplete List of Sometimes Unexpected but Increasingly Common Credit Card Fees

Balance Transfer Fee

Have you ever been invited to move a debt from one credit card to another at zero percent "introductory" interest? Have you ever wondered how a credit card company can make money that way? One big part of the answer: by imposing a balance transfer fee (typically, 3 percent of the total, with a $5 to $10 minimum) large enough to render the introductory interest rate meaningless.[32]

Cash Advance Fee

The interest rate on cash advances is usually higher than it is for purchases; often it's as high as 20 or 25 percent.[33] But once again, it's not the whole story; most credit companies charge a fee of 1 to 4 percent as well.

Foreign Exchange or International Fees

Travelers, take note: Your card may be accepted all over, but card companies now commonly charge a foreign-transaction fee—typically in the neighborhood of 3 percent, according to a recent report by the General Accounting Office.[34]

Late Fee

Are you one of those people who have trouble remember-
ing the important dates in your life? If so, you may be the
ideal customer in the credit card industry's eyes. Late fees—
largely nonexistent until about fifteen years ago—have increased from an average of $13 in 1995 to $34 today.[35]

Late fees (not to be confused with penalty interest rates,
which generally kick in at the same time) are not only bigger than ever; they get levied sooner than ever. Credit card
companies now commonly impose fees whenever a payment arrives after a specified time of day.

issuers charging 30 percent or more.[36] Many credit card companies now start counting a payment as late if it comes after a certain
time of day. (In one survey of card practices, only three banks—
comparatively small ones—were found to not have penalty rates
on their cards.)[37]

Many banks now assert the right to raise interest rates for reasons they need not specify in advance. Like Santa Claus, who "sees
you when you're sleeping" and "knows when you're awake," credit
card issuers are watching over their cardholders' financial conduct
and making adjustments in response to things like a late or
bounced payment to another creditor or even a casual inquiry
about a potentially unwise loan.

In March 2007, Citibank renounced this practice, known as
"universal default." Other banks, however, have stuck with it, and

the broader enthusiasm for what Elizabeth Warren calls "tricks and traps" continues unabated. All told, Americans now spend about $90 billion annually in interest and penalty payments on credit cards, or more than $800 per cardholding household.[38]

"Making people pay for access to credit is a lucrative business wherever it is practiced," Kahr observed in another of his legendary memos. "Is any bit of food too small to grab when you're starving and when there is nothing else in sight? The trick is charging a lot, repeatedly, for small doses of incremental credit."[39] Or, as he put it in yet another memo (this time he could almost have been proposing a motto for the credit card industry as a whole), the idea is "to squeeze out enough revenue and get customers to sit still for the squeeze."[40]

RACE TO THE BOTTOM

The credit card industry has often been accused of collusive pricing, and it's easy to see why such a suspicion might arise. In 1995, the top ten card issuers controlled slightly more than half the market; by 2006, their share was closing in on 90 percent. Two organizations, Visa and MasterCard, together account for about 80 percent of the transaction-processing end of the business. While their client banks control other pricing decisions, Visa and MasterCard themselves set the so-called interchange fees, the service charges paid by merchants. Retailer organizations have complained bitterly and repeatedly over these fees, which have doubled since 1995 despite technological advances that (merchants argue) should have made the credit card business more efficient.

In 2005, interchange fees ranged between 1.6 and 1.7 percent, generating more than $30 billion in revenue.[41]

Long the most profitable area of banking, credit cards enjoy a return on assets more than three times that of commercial banking in general. In 2006, the industry earned an estimated $36.8 billion in profits, up nearly 80 percent from its 2000 level.[42] For example, according to Citigroup's SEC filings, the company's consumer lending business—encompassing such things as home mortgages, auto loans, and student loans—had a return on assets, or net profit, of 0.79 percent. The return on Citigroup's credit card lending business that year was 6.17 percent![43] The tricks and traps that characterize the credit card business model generate robust profits, far greater than the profits derived from other areas of lending, largely because it is so woefully underregulated.

While price-fixing may be a worry, it is not the only one. Over the past twenty-five years, the typical credit card agreement has expanded from one page to more than thirty pages, with the contract language often spread over multiple documents and not easily distinguished from reams of other verbiage.[44] Most agreements are written at a tenth- to twelfth-grade reading level, although half the population reads at or below an eighth-grade level.[45] Indeed, it is debatable whether any level of reading comprehension qualifies someone to wade through the thicket of fees, penalties, contingent interest rates, and legalisms of these contracts.

Can there really be such a thing as a free market or an informed consumer in a situation like this? A number of people who have studied the workings of the credit card industry have concluded that there can't be. Credit cards belong to a class of extremely complex pricing scenarios, Oren Bar-Gill argued in his 2004 monograph, "Seduction by Plastic," where a sophisticated seller will almost invariably get the better of an individual buyer.[46] In the lending field, this general problem may be compounded by the habitual tendency of borrowers to underestimate future, as opposed to present, financial difficulties. This "optimism bias," as some have termed it, produces decisions based on the up-front and obvious costs, as opposed to those that arise later and depend on certain contingencies of borrower behavior. Credit card companies routinely take advantage of the optimism bias, Ronald J. Mann writes in his book *Charging Ahead: The Growth and Regulation of Payment Card Markets.* They "identify a myopic class of customers and exploit the lack of rationality by systematically backloading the less attractive terms into a less prominent time and place in the relationship."[47]

Bar-Gill points out that "instead of bringing down interest rates and eliminating late and over-the-limit fees, competition is focused only on short-term perks." Consumers are encouraged to ignore the most dangerous costs—the ones that hit them when they are most vulnerable.[48] Competition can lead the managers of some companies to adopt practices that have improved the balance sheets of others, even if they never would have thought of those practices on their own. In other words, competition, far from being the solution, is part of the problem.

HERE, KITTY, KITTY . . .

Since 1970, it has been illegal to send credit cards to people who have not requested them. But while that law may have cut down

MANY REVENUE STREAMS =
ONE BIG TORRENT OF REVENUE

Credit card issuers make money in six basic ways. Here's
how it all broke down in 2005.

Interest	$ 71.13 billion
Interchange fees	20.62 billion
Penalty fees	7.88 billion
Cash advance fees	5.26 billion
Annual fees	3.26 billion
Enhancements	0.85 billion
Total	$109.00 billion

Cards & Payments, reproduced in Bank Card Profitability,
2005–2004, CardWeb (2006).

slightly on the amount of plastic that people receive in the mail,
the volume of paper churned out by the industry has kept right on
growing. In 2006, credit card offers—including "preapproved"
applications—added up to an estimated 8 billion pieces of direct
mail.[49]

No industry pushes its product harder, and these days it is difficult to find any sign of the old skittishness about fraud and default. In February 2007, Bank of America announced plans to
issue a credit card designed expressly for undocumented aliens.[50]
(It has yet to move forward with that plan, possibly because of
some uneasiness expressed by immigration officials.) With "risk-

based pricing," virtually all Americans are now seen as potential cardholders. But if the industry has singled out any one group for the greatest attention, it is the young—college students in particular.

Many Americans have their first encounter with the lending industry at freshman orientation, where credit card sales operatives can be found stationed at booths and tables, handing out Frisbees, T-shirts, and other goodies along with their application forms. Chase, in one recent year, offered free pedicab rides to any University of Michigan student willing to listen to an advertisement while cruising around the town of Ann Arbor.[51] The first visit to the campus bookstore becomes another opportunity to sign up for a card. Even more solicitations can be found pinned to bulletin boards or on popular Web sites like Facebook.com.[52]

Colleges and universities are in part to blame for the presence and prevalence of lenders on college campuses. Lenders are spending millions of dollars each year in contracts with colleges and universities to set up shop on campuses and solicit the highly profitable youth market.[53] In 2000, for example, First USA Bank (now Bank One) struck a $16.5 million deal with the University of Tennessee in Knoxville in exchange for contact information for students, associates, and alumni.[54] First USA had similar deals in as many as two hundred schools nationwide in 2002.[55]

For the credit card companies, the investment has paid off nicely. According to a study by Nellie Mae, three-quarters of all undergraduates use credit cards for school supplies (paper, notebooks, etc.), and nearly as many use them for textbooks. One in four students use their cards to help pay for tuition.[56] Gone are the days when minors had to get their parents to cosign a credit card application. In fact, savvy lenders would rather not have adults know too much; students make more use of their cards, the industry has found, when their parents are kept in the dark. According to the same survey, more than 90 percent of college seniors have at least one credit card, and many don't stop at one.[57] In 2004, the average senior had five cards and carried an average balance of $2,864. Almost one-quarter of students had credit card debt greater than $3,000.

The marketing of credit cards on college campuses has become a sensitive topic in Washington, with legislators frequently hinting at a crackdown. Meanwhile, the industry has pressed forward with efforts to reach an even younger demographic. In 2000, Visa began marketing a prepaid debit card called the Visa Buxx, "specially designed to offer teens spending independence and responsibility, while keeping parents informed, involved and in control."[58] Not to be outdone, MasterCard pitched its Hello Kitty debit card to high school and even junior high students.[59] (Prepaid debit cards have been viewed by some in the industry as a way to get teenagers adjusted to using credit cards.) "We think our target age group will be from 10 to 14, although it could certainly go younger," said Bruce Giuliano, senior vice president of licensing for Sanrio Inc., which owns the Hello Kitty brand.[60]

4

MORTGAGE MAYHEM

Before Al Ynigues started high school, people knew what he would do for a living, because he was doing it already—singing, composing, and playing guitar and drums for family, friends, and neighbors in his hometown of San Angelo, Texas. Ynigues made his professional debut at the age of twelve, winning a local "battle of the bands" as part of a group called Al and the Bluenotes. Now in his sixties, he has performed with Duke Ellington, Count Basie, and Kris Kristofferson over the years, and he has taught music to hundreds of students in the suburbs of Minneapolis–St. Paul since he moved there in 1994.

It was one of his adult students—a mortgage broker—who got Ynigues thinking about becoming a homeowner. In 2004, after a lifetime of renting, Ynigues bought a three-bedroom house in Apple Valley, a picture-postcard suburb twenty minutes south of Minneapolis. The upstairs became his living quarters. Downstairs, Ynigues set up one room for percussion lessons, one for piano lessons, and one for his recording studio and instrument-repair work.

It was a happy outcome for Ynigues. It was also the kind of

story that bankers and lenders like to tell to illustrate the benefits of deregulation. For until recently, they point out, someone in Ynigues's position—self-employed with an unpredictable income and a sketchy credit history—would not have stood much chance of getting a mortgage.[1]

SUBPRIME SUPERHEROES

Banks and savings and loans used to have the mortgage business to themselves. If you wanted to buy a house and needed a loan, you had to convince one of these institutions that you and your property added up to a safe bet. Getting approved was a rite of passage into the middle class. With housing prices spiraling upward, it was often a step toward economic security in its own right—the beginning of a story that could almost be counted on to end with the words "and they lived happily ever after."

But many people were not approved, and many knew better than to apply. In addition to a first mortgage covering 80 percent of the price of his house, Ynigues received a form of second mortgage known as a "piggyback loan" for the balance.[2] Piggyback loans, which have become an industry unto themselves, scarcely existed as recently as a decade ago. To qualify for a mortgage, you had to make a down payment of 20 percent or more. Ynigues didn't have kind of money. Even if he had, some loan officers might have rated him a borderline applicant, and as a Latino, there was a good chance that he would not have received the benefit of the doubt.

Because many communities had only a few banks, a relatively small number of people held the power to decide who would receive a mortgage and who wouldn't. In Minnesota and elsewhere, most of these decision makers were white males and most of the loan money went to people who looked like them.[3]

Discriminatory lending—against women, people of color, and others—was a huge problem. It remained a problem even after the passage of three major pieces of reform legislation in the 1960s and 1970s. The Fair Housing Act of 1968 barred landlords, real estate companies, and others from discriminating on the basis of race, religion, national origin, gender, family status, or disability. The Equal Credit Opportunity Act (ECOA) of 1974 extended those principles to lenders, and the Community Reinvestment Act of 1977 called on banks to devote a portion of their resources to the credit needs of low- and moderate-income neighborhoods. (A fourth measure, the Home Mortgage Disclosure Act of 1975, gave watchdog agencies and community groups the ability to monitor how this or that bank was doing.)[4]

These laws made a difference. Even so, the complaints continued, and lenders began to argue that the answer lay in fewer rules, not more. Regulation, they said, had effectively limited them to one kind of mortgage, and therefore to one kind of borrower. To serve a wider range of people, industry leaders insisted, they needed the freedom to consider different levels of risk and set their loan terms accordingly.

They got some of that freedom from the Depository Institutions Deregulation and Monetary Act of 1980, which allowed higher-interest loans. They got more from the Alternative Mortgage Party Transaction Act of 1982, which paved the way for piggyback loans, interest-only loans, adjustable-rate loans, and other features commonly found in today's subprime mortgages.[5]

Another decade passed, however, before the subprime mortgage business got off the ground. That happened through the efforts of a group of mortgage specialty companies that entered the field in the 1990s after the breakdown of the savings and loan industry. With no deposits to draw on, these so-called nonbank lenders had to come up with another means of financing. Taking their cue from the government-sponsored mortgage entities known as Freddie Mac, Fannie Mae, and Ginnie Mae, some nonbank lenders began working with Wall Street investment banks to bundle their loans into securities and sell them to investors. Through this process of "securitization," they tapped into a vast new pool of capital, which led to a tremendous increase in lending.[6]

Between 1994 and 2005, the annual total of subprime home loans increased from $35 billion to $665 billion.[7] The approval rate for minority applicants rose, too: from 40 percent to over 70 percent in the case of African Americans; from 58 percent to nearly 80 percent in the case of Latinos.[8] So the industry had some impressive numbers to cite in support of its case for "risk-based lending" as a tool of economic opportunity. But that was not always how it felt to the people on the receiving end.

EXPLODING ARMS

Al Ynigues didn't know much about mortgages. Nevertheless, he knew enough to ask his broker for a thirty-year fixed-interest loan—and enough to feel uneasy when, at the last minute, he learned that he would be getting an adjustable-rate mortgage instead. His broker said this was nothing to worry about, though. While his interest rate might go up "a little," Ynigues remembered being told, "sometimes the mortgage rates go down, and if they go down, you'll pay less."

As it turned out, his interest rate went up. In October 2006, his combined monthly payments rose from a barely manageable $2,100 to a dicey $2,417. Ynigues's income had slipped in the meantime. Now he would have to devote almost every penny to house payments. Even if he managed to keep up, Ynigues calculated, he would be doing little better than covering the interest.[9]

In the subprime mortgage business, Ynigues would find out, things were not always as they appeared. An adjustable rate, for example. It certainly sounded like one that would rise or fall with inflation, and adjustable-rate loans, or ARMs, usually did operate that way in the prime end of the mortgage market. Like many other subprime borrowers, however, Ynigues had received a so-called 2/28 loan, which started off with two years of fixed interest, followed by twenty-eight years of adjustments (at six-month intervals). Among lending rights advocates, they were known as "exploding ARMs" because of a detail that the adjustable-rate label helped conceal: the initial rate was a teaser rate, set so low as to guarantee a sharp rise at the two-year mark, regardless of inflation.[10]

Ynigues's rate hike was actually fairly modest compared to the increases that some people faced. In Detroit around the same time, Jennifer Moore's monthly payment went from $1,450 to $2,200. The recently widowed Moore, who had a clerical job with the county government, had been a homeowner for more than thirty years. By the spring of 2007, she was behind on her payments and resigned to losing her home.[11]

Subprime mortgages were complicated, and the complications

usually served to hide their true cost. Unlike traditional mortgage lenders, most subprime lenders did not ask borrowers to put money in escrow for taxes or insurance. These charges, like the so-called adjustable rate, kicked in later. Unanticipated tax and escrow costs helped explain the 40 percent payment increase that hit Jennie Haliburton after she took out a refinancing loan on her Philadelphia home in 2006. Her initial mortgage payment of $922 was a stretch but doable on her $1,766 monthly Social Security; a year later, she was facing a monthly payment of nearly $1,300— about 70 percent of her income.[12]

Refinancing loans like Haliburton's accounted for more than half of all subprime mortgages.[13] Many people used them to pay off credit card debts and lower their interest payments. Like credit card agreements, though, subprime mortgages often carried unexpected fees and interest-rate hikes—unexpected by the borrower, that is, but carefully engineered by the lender.

In Chicago, a telemarketer convinced Delores King, a seventy-year-old retiree, to refinance her home in February 2005. King started off at $832 a month—slightly more than she had been paying on her old mortgage. But her loan turned out to have an unusually low teaser rate, lasting just a few months. King's payments quickly jumped to $1,488—more than her monthly income. Her motivation for taking out the loan in the first place had been to pay off credit card debts of about $3,000.[14]

PUSHING AND STEERING

Borrowers used to do business with lenders directly. Now, increasingly, they dealt with mortgage brokers, and many would come to realize that, like the word "adjustable," the word "broker" had developed a meaning of its own in the subprime mortgage universe. Normally, the term suggests an intermediary or a facilitator: someone in the business of bringing two parties together and trying to do right by both. That was not how many subprime mortgage brokers saw themselves, however. Their income came from commissions, and their commissions basically depended on two things—the loan amount and the interest rate. Like the lending companies they worked with, brokers had a powerful economic motivation to issue as many loans as possible, and to make every loan as large and as costly as possible for the borrower.[15]

The bank loan officers of old sat at desks and waited for customers to come to them. Subprime mortgage brokers went out looking for customers. Going into neighborhoods that banks had shunned, they were the industry's shock troops in a massive "push-marketing" campaign. They knocked on doors; they passed out fliers; they telemarketed; they networked at church picnics and community meetings. And when they found a prospect, most brokers did not spend a vast amount of time explaining the costs and perils of the product.[16]

Balloon payments, prepayment penalties, high interest rates, unusual closing costs—many subprime loans came with charges like these, and many borrowers failed to notice. "Things My Broker Never Really Told Me" could be the title of a hefty collection of subprime stories. One of the most widespread forms of deception, however, has continued to go largely unrecognized: a great many of those who received subprime mortgages (about 20 percent, according to an analysis of loans issued in 2003 and 2004) could have qualified for traditional mortgages, had they only known.[17] And ignorance was expensive. Mortgages generally come with up-front charges known as points; in the subprime world, the norm was about 3 percent of the loan amount, compared to 1 percent or less for a conventional fixed-rate mortgage. With a $150,000 loan, in other words, the subprime borrower would be paying an extra $4,500 or so at the outset. The higher interest rates of subprime loans meant that the cost difference would only grow with time. In 2005, the interest on a typical adjustable-rate subprime mortgage worked out to the annual equivalent of 7.5 percent—compared to the prime-mortgage average of about 6 percent. Over seven years of payments, that would mean another $8,000.[18]

Minority applicants were especially likely to be steered into needlessly expensive loans. One explanation emerged in a 2007 report by a team of Harvard University housing market researchers. African Americans, having lived through the era of redlining, were often pleasantly surprised to learn that they could get credit at all. Many never suspected that they might be eligible for lower-cost loans than the ones they were offered. In some cases, people assumed that the terms of a loan were dictated by a rigorous process, with brokers or loan officers sitting down and reviewing an applicant's finances based "on a set of standard criteria."[19]

And so, while blacks and Latinos were getting more mortgages, they were particularly likely to end up with exploding ARMs and other expensive and tricky loans, even if they had credit records that ought to have entitled them to something better.[20] Even many upper-income blacks and Latinos got steered into subprime mortgages. (It happened to upper-income whites as well, but less than half as often.)[21]

Before he bought his house, Al Ynigues heard about a subsidized loan program for first-time homeowners. The program had been developed by ACORN, a national organization of low- and moderate-income families, in partnership with banks seeking to meet their Community Reinvestment Act obligations.[22] ACORN's program could have been a godsend to Ynigues, as it has been to tens of thousands of others. But when he brought it up, according to Ynigues, his broker "completely discouraged me."[23]

Across the country, other borrowers had the same experience; brokers would tell them that subsidized loan programs "take too long" or "require too much paperwork."[24] Very few brokers seem to have mentioned another consideration: subprime lenders paid far bigger commissions than traditional lenders did; in addition, with subprime loans, brokers usually received a form of legal kickback known as a "yield spread premium"—a direct payment from the lender based on the amount of interest the borrower had agreed to pay *above* the minimum that the loan company would have approved.[25] The yield spread premium was, in the words of Prentiss Cox, a University of Minnesota law professor who had worked on mortgage fraud cases as a state prosecutor, "a payment for giving homeowners a worse deal."[26]

Ynigues would eventually learn that his broker had received a yield spread premium of $5,000.[27] It was just one of many pieces of information he would have liked to have had *before* he signed his loan papers.

THE GOLD RUSH TRAIL

Irv Ackelsberg, a prominent lending rights lawyer in Philadelphia, has compared the subprime mortgage boom to a gold rush, the gold in this case being the home equity wealth of neighborhoods and population groups that the lending industry had previously undervalued.[28] While there was no precise moment of discovery, 2004 was a breakout year for the industry. By now, the major Wall Street firms, including Merrill Lynch, Lehman Brothers, and Bear Stearns, were in the business of packaging subprime mortgage securities and selling them to "yield-hungry investors around the world," as the *Wall Street Journal*'s Michael Hudson put it.[29]

What could be a better deal, many investors reasoned, than a loan product with higher-than-average interest to begin with— and rigged to go even higher? There was risk, to be sure, but the risk had been carefully calibrated and fully taken into account, or so the experts all seemed to agree.[30] No less an authority than the chairman of the Federal Reserve, Alan Greenspan, had paid tribute to the lending industry's remarkable new ability (as he said in a 2004 speech) to "quite efficiently judge the risk posed by individual applicants and to price that risk appropriately."[31]

Ynigues's loan came from a company called New Century. One of the pioneers in the field, New Century built up a network of tens of thousands of brokers, who appreciated its generous commissions and speedy approval process. Thanks to its Fast Qual loan software, a broker could go online and in a mere twelve seconds (the company boasted) know whether an application was likely to get through. New Century was popular on Wall Street, too. The company had developed a warm relationship with the investment banking firm of Morgan Stanley, which helped underwrite nearly $10 billion of New Century's mortgage-backed securities, reaping some $17.4 million for its services.[32]

While Ynigues and others were falling behind on their payments and beginning to worry about losing their homes, salespeople and account executives at New Century could look forward to festive gatherings in far-flung places: one big company bash took place in a train station in Barcelona, another on a yacht in the Bahamas. At the height of the subprime boom, New Century had so much money lying around that it was able to sponsor a NASCAR race and send some of its top-performing people to a Porsche racing school.[33] One high-level executive, according to the *Wall Street Journal*, finished the year 2004 with more than $4 million in compensation. (In 2005, the company gave him a six-month leave of absence at the comparatively modest pay of $76,445 a month while he "looked for new horizons," as the *Journal* put it.)[34]

With investors clamoring for more securities and lenders stepping up their efforts to deliver, tens of thousands of people decided to try their luck in the subprime goldfields. Taher Afghani, a Southern Californian in his midtwenties, made his move after a chance encounter with a high-spirited group of young brokers on a weekend jaunt to Mexico. It wasn't anything they said about the work that caught his interest; it was how much money they had and how freely they spent it. They had "the best clothes, the cars, the girls, everything," Afghani explained later to a reporter for *Bloomberg News*.

Afghani went to a work for Secured Funding, another big non-bank lender, as one of a thousand salespeople operating out of an 80,000-square-foot facility in Costa Mesa, California. During their long workdays, their fancy vehicles filled up such a big swath of the neighborhood that one of Afghani's colleagues took to using an electric scooter for the commute from her office to her parked car.[35] With no experience, Afghani earned $120,000 in his first year as a broker—more than twice what he had made in his previous job managing a Target warehouse.[36]

You didn't make that kind of money with a softspoken manner or a balanced presentation. In their sales pitches, Afghani and others learned to focus on the benefits, not the costs. The industry took the same approach in its marketing; ads for refinancing loans encouraged people to think about the many fine things they could do with a little extra money—remodel a kitchen, buy a car, or consolidate other debts into "one easy payment."[37] Rapid approval was another big theme. In TV and radio ads, billboards, and barrages of direct mail, the message was: "Bad credit OK." "Need cash? Fast Approvals." "Banks Say No, We Say Yes."[38]

In the past, getting a mortgage had generally been the borrower's idea. Now, it was often the broker's idea. In a survey of older borrowers with refinancing loans, the AARP found that the broker or lender had initiated the contact in more than 60 percent of cases. Over half had responded to advertisements or phone calls. Most of these loans, the AARP concluded, were "sold, not sought."[39] As *Bloomberg* reporters Seth Lubove and Daniel Taub summed it up, the broker's mission (at Secured Funding and a good many other companies) "was to reel in borrowers, period. Never mind whether customers needed loans or could manage payments."[40]

Secured Funding invested heavily in direct mail. The idea was not simply to advertise the availability of loan money but to identify the easiest prospects: people who would be receptive to the idea of a loan, and, at the same time, not too inquisitive about the terms. In one of its mailings, the company enclosed fake $75,000 checks with the reassuring message that "Less Than Perfect Credit Is OK!" Another packet contained a "personalized Platinum Equity Card" offering "$50,000 or more in cash" to anyone who took the trouble to call a toll-free number.[41]

STREAM OF WIDOWS

As they spread the industry gospel of credit for those who had been denied credit in the past, brokers and lenders steered a striking number of prime mortgage candidates into subprime mortgages. And by the final stages of the subprime boom, a large proportion of their loans were going to people who were in no position to repay them—other than through foreclosure or a forced sale.

Patricia Tamillo was a cerebral palsy patient living on a $569-a-month disability check. The Milwaukee broker who handled her refinancing loan had to know she was disabled—Tamillo was in a wheelchair when they met. Nevertheless, she was approved for a $77,000 mortgage and listed in the loan papers as a "handy-woman" making $20,000 a year. "They said I'd save $300 a month and get $3,000 cash out," Tamillo said later. "To a person who's broke, that sounds pretty good." By March 2007, Tamillo's house, which she had inherited from her mother, was in foreclosure.[42]

Tamillo's case was extreme—but only slightly. Many borrowers would tell parallel stories about reading over the mortgage paperwork and finding that their incomes had been put down at double or triple the reality, or that they had been given invented jobs or occupations. In Atlanta, one public-interest lawyer's clients and would-be clients included, he said later, "a stream of elderly widows whose Social Security incomes [had] been padded—on paper—by made-up jobs."[43]

As the number of subprime mortgages rose, so did the rate of delinquency. Foreclosure proceedings set a record of 847,000 in 2005, before jumping to 1.2 million the following year.[44] Complaints of mortgage fraud increased fourteenfold between 1997 and 2005. During that time, more than eighty thousand fraud complaints were logged by the federal Financial Crimes Enforcement Network.[45]

Like the adjustable-rate mortgage, the interest-only loan with a balloon payment had been a niche product, reserved for comparatively well-off borrowers and special circumstances. By 2006, such loans accounted for roughly one-quarter of the mortgage market. Almost half the home-purchase mortgages issued that year were so-called stated income or no-doc loans, in which borrowers were not required to supply tax returns or other evidence of their finances—"liar's loans," many industry insiders called them matter-of-factly.[46]

Appraisals and loan amounts climbed to record heights. In 2000, according to Bank of America Securities, the average subprime loan was equal to 48 percent of the appraised value of the property; by 2006, it was 82 percent.[47] Long before the subprime industry went into its final meltdown, in other words, the signs of looming disaster were clear to all who cared to see—clear, that is, to all except the brokers, lenders, securities packagers, and others who continued to reap the profits, and most of the public officials who should have been watching over them.

MELTDOWN

In December 2006, federal prosecutors were alerted to some curious numbers in New Century's financial reports. The rate of missed mortgage payments had gone up sharply; 2.5 percent of the latest borrowers had not even sent in a first-month check—a well-known indicator of fraud in the mortgage world. Meanwhile, the company had reduced the size of its reserve fund—a strange move unless, as prosecutors may have begun to suspect, the idea was to maintain an appearance of steady profitability while insiders began to unload their stock. Five New Century directors and officers sold shares worth about $29 million that year; most of the sales occurred between August and November, while share prices remained high.[48]

Two months later, when New Century announced that it had become the target of a federal investigation, lending-industry leaders rushed to distance themselves from its practices. Kurt Pfotenhauer, principal Washington lobbyist for the Mortgage Bankers Association, drew a sharp distinction between the bottom-feeders to be found in any field and the reputable elements of what he called a "fundamentally honest" business that was "trying to offer a product that's good and useful to borrowers who are asking for it." "There are always a few," Pfotenhauer said, "who will deliberately go out and try to deceive."[49]

But in the subprime mortgage business, there were way more than a few, and some of those bottom-feeders had swiftly matured into very big fish. By the time New Century filed for Chapter 11 bankruptcy protection at the beginning of April 2007, it was one of two dozen lenders that had ceased operations with or without that legal formality. New Century alone issued some $60 billion worth of loans in 2006. On the eve of its collapse, the company had two hundred branch offices and a network of some forty-seven thousand brokers.[50]

It wasn't just a group of companies going under. It was virtually the whole subprime mortgage industry. In California alone, some twelve thousand jobs disappeared during the first five months of 2007. Twenty-eight percent of Ohio's mortgage brokerage firms failed to renew their licenses, and 16 percent went out of business. In Minnesota, the first six months of 2007 saw nearly ninety brokerage companies surrender their licenses, according to the state Department of Commerce; others would let their licenses lapse without bothering to notify the state.[51]

Soon there were disturbing announcements from more mainstream quarters of the financial world. Morgan Stanley, Lehman Brothers, and Merrill Lynch all reported steep losses due largely or in part to subprime mortgage holdings. The Swiss banking giant UBS closed down a hedge fund after its manager lost $124 million.[52] Bear Stearns had to set aside $1.6 billion to shore up one of two hedge funds that had nearly been wiped out by subprime losses.[53] Wells Fargo, a major subprime lender, announced the elimination of more than five hundred jobs.[54] The ripple effects reached as far as General Motors, whose profits for the first quarter of 2007 fell sharply as a result of losses at a subprime subsidiary of GMAC, the auto-financing company that GM half-owned.[55]

The trouble spread because the recklessness and duplicity had spread. Citigroup, for example, was one of a number of large banks that kept their subprime and prime lending operations rigorously separate. Citigroup's subprime subsidiary, CitiFinancial, had its own offices, staff, and practices. Like other subprime mortgage companies, CitiFinancial was push-marketing high-priced loans in minority communities, with no provision to redirect qualified applicants to lower-priced mortgages issued by the corporate parent. In 2001, pressure from consumer organizations led Citigroup to announce a "referral up" program that was supposed to address this problem, but the requirements were so strict that they continued to exclude many people who might have been approved for prime loans if they had applied for them directly.[56] (In 2002, Citigroup agreed to pay more than $200 million to settle a Federal Trade Commission predatory-lending complaint; CitiFinancial, according to the FTC, had been "packing" mortgage contracts with unwanted credit insurance and other services, and counting on borrowers to overlook the charges.)[57]

HSBC became a subprime lender through the purchase of Household Finance, a company that had paid $484 million to settle a predatory-lending lawsuit brought by all fifty state attorney generals.[58] HSBC was also a major packager of subprime loans for other lenders, including Secured Funding, which had some of the edgiest practices in the business. Perhaps unsurprisingly, HSBC's mortgage portfolio turned out to include a large number of no-doc loans. In February 2007, HSBC announced that it had set aside nearly $11 billion to cover anticipated losses in the subprime market.[59]

Liar's loans, inflated appraisals, outlandish fees, serial refinancing, bait-and-switch marketing—all these practices were well on the way to becoming the mortgage-lending norm when the roof came crashing down. If the line between predatory lending and subprime lending had become blurred, it was the industry itself that had done most of the blurring.

WINNERS AND LOSERS

After the meltdown came the damage assessment. By the first quarter of 2007, 5 percent of existing subprime mortgages were in foreclosure and nearly 16 percent were delinquent.[60] With a million subprime borrowers awaiting their first interest-rate "resets" in 2007, and another eight hundred thousand facing that prospect in 2008, predictions were bound to be iffy.[61] Nevertheless, many lenders insisted that the number of foreclosures and forced sales would fall short of the 2.2 million estimate put forward by the Center for Responsible Lending.[62] In any case, the great majority of borrowers would not default, so the winners, the industry said, would far outnumber the losers.

Outside observers came to the same conclusion. "Yeah, people got bad mortgages. But others were able to finally buy a home," was how *Time* magazine put it.[63] The editorial page of the *Richmond Times-Dispatch* pointed out that without subprime mortgages, "these folks would still be renters. . . . And nearly everyone agrees that expanding the number of homeowners is a good thing—for the new homeowners, for the economy, and for society."[64]

In economics, wisdom is often associated with an ability to set emotions aside, tote up the gains and losses, and see the "big picture." But the big picture is not always a clear picture. Sometimes the experts need to come down from the clouds and take a look at real life—the real lives of people like, say, Stephen DiPhilippo and his extended family in Stoneham, north of Boston.

DiPhilippo and his father both worked in the construction trade, and they had a heavy investment of sweat equity in the seven-bedroom house where three generations of DiPhilippos lived. When his father decided to retire, Stephen DiPhilippo (as he told National Public Radio later) went to see a broker with the idea of buying the house. Since he did not have a regular paycheck, his broker suggested a no-doc loan. DiPhilippo went along because he was quoted an interest rate of 5.9 percent. It was only on the day before closing, he said, that he learned that the interest would be 8.5 percent. By then, his father was embroiled in a dispute with the existing mortgage holder, so "they had us over a barrel."

The DiPhilippos went forward with the loan after a conversation with their broker that led them to believe they would have little trouble refinancing at a lower interest rate later on. As it turned out, they had a lot of trouble, and by then their mortgage payments, which had started out at $2,300 a month, were approaching $4,000. By the homeownership yardstick, however, the DiPhilippos could be counted as winners, since they did manage to refinance in the end, after months of anxiety and tens of thousands of dollars in excess interest and fees—money that was not available to advance other life goals, such as college for their children.[65]

The rise and fall of the subprime mortgage industry is a story that needs to be placed in context—as part of the three-decades-long American experience of soaring home prices and soaring debt. Over that time, homeownership became a route to economic well-being and even affluence for millions of families. Many who bought homes with subprime mortgages no doubt hoped to follow in their path; lenders and brokers took advantage of that hope, even as they helped create a market that made its fulfillment increasingly unlikely.

The formula had never been as surefire as it seemed. To do really well in the housing market, you need to take optimal advantage of the income tax deductions for mortgage interest and local property tax payments; these deductions, like all deductions, yield large rewards for high-income families, and progressively less economic benefit for those lower down the ladder.

Subprime lenders compounded the problem by saddling people with excessive and needlessly expensive debt—and by driving home prices higher. Into an already bubbly housing market, subprime lenders, and the investors and Wall Streeters who bankrolled them, pumped another big blast of froth. By doing so, they increased the pool of prospective buyers and the sums of money that people could supposedly afford to pay. Between 2000 and 2005, home prices went up 50 percent, from an average of $119,600 to $167,500.[66]

A booming housing market can be a fine thing for people who buy early in the cycle, and sell late; it is not so wonderful for those who come along toward the end, especially in a hot real estate market like, say, Boston, where by 2006 the median-income family could afford the median-priced home in only 12 of 161 metropolitan-area communities. (As recently as 1998, the median-income family could afford the median-priced home in 148 of those communities.)[67]

Homeownership is not a magic formula for economic opportunity, certainly not when it is achieved with dangerous levels of debt. Many who bought homes with subprime mortgages would have been better off renting—and many people who held onto their homes would clearly have been better off if they had kept their original mortgages. By the end, the subprime mortgage market had taken on the character of a Ponzi scheme, in which a pattern of spectacular short-term gains rests on an ever-increasing intake of investment. It is hard to predict exactly when these situations will end; the one thing you can say for sure is that when they do, a relatively small number of people will be richer—and a much larger number will be poorer.

THE BIGGER PICTURE

The subprime mortgage industry had trained its marketing efforts on a particular set of communities and populations. Now those same communities and populations would bear a disproportionate share of the harm. This would be the experience not only of African Americans and Latinos, but of Native Americans, rural Americans, and the elderly. In the Cleveland suburb of Euclid, more than six hundred houses had been through foreclosure by early 2007; many were the homes of elderly people who, after refinancing with two-year teaser rates, had been hit with payment increases of 50 percent or more.[68]

On a single block of West Outer Drive in Detroit—where Aretha Franklin, Marvin Gaye, and Berry Gordy, founder of Motown, had once lived—the owners of seven of twenty-six homes had taken out subprime loans; three families were already facing eviction. Big red refuse bins sat outside several nearby houses; the bins had been put there by banks, which were emptying out the contents in an effort to make the houses more sellable. But few people expected a rush of buyers. As one local realtor commented, "Nobody's going to want to buy into a neighborhood with 20 percent foreclosures."[69]

From a distance, the foreclosure problem might seem comparatively modest. It certainly didn't look that way in Cleveland or Detroit, or in sections of Atlanta, Philadelphia, Cincinnati, Charlotte, Memphis, or Cedar Knolls, New Jersey, where local homeless programs were unable to accommodate all the people who had lost homes and had nowhere to go; some foreclosure victims were living in their cars, according to a local credit counselor.[70]

In these "pockets of pain," as reporter Steve Tripoli of National Public Radio called them, the meltdown also affected people who had never taken out a subprime mortgage in the first place. Foreclosures mean lost taxes and added maintenance costs for local governments; a municipality can end up paying tens of thousands of dollars for a single foreclosure.[71] "We are looking at hundreds of thousands of dollars being sucked out of a community that could desperately use that money to build wealth, to fix the roads, to send the kids to better schools," said Diane Thompson, a legal services lawyer in East St. Louis, Illinois, where by the spring of 2007 a foreclosed home stood on almost every corner. "And instead, that money is just disappearing in exorbitant credit rates."[72]

When foreclosure rates rise, property values fall. Business investment and tax revenues also suffer.[73] That is to say nothing of consequences that are more difficult to express in dollars: a child shifted from one school to another; a family separated from its roots. In Detroit, as Jennifer Moore prepared to move into an apartment, she was saying good-bye to the porch she had had built to take in the sun and the library she had decked out with her son's baseball and basketball trophies."[74] Such things don't always show up in the economic "big picture."

Counting up winners and losers based on who still had a home was certainly not the best way to gauge the impact of the subprime mortgage boom. And yet, even by that narrow standard, the impact would have turned out to be a negative one. Most of the homeownership gains, the Center for Responsible Lending documented in a 2007 report, had occurred during the 1990s, *before* the surge of subprime mortgages. The gains had been driven by other forces, most obviously by a strong economy; the Community Reinvestment Act had played a part, accounting for some 336,000 home purchase loans to low- and moderate-income Americans between 1993 and 2000, according to another study.[75]

The great majority of subprime loans had been for refinancing, not for home purchases. Between 2001 and 2006, Americans cashed out an estimated $1.2 trillion in home equity.[76] So while more people "owned" homes, most people owned less of their homes. (Total homeowner equity has been on a downward slide for decades, falling from 68.3 percent in 1973 to 55 percent as of 2004.)[77]

In fact, less than 10 percent of all the subprime loans originated between 1998 and 2006 had gone to first-time home buyers. That added up to an estimated 1.4 million people—a figure that, as Michael Calhoun, executive director of the Center for Responsible Lending, pointed out, was far exceeded by the number of subprime borrowers who lost homes through foreclosure over the same period. In the name of homeownership, the lending industry had come up with a set of products and practices that, in Calhoun's words, had "been thwarting homeownership rather than supporting it."[78]

5

ASLEEP AT THE SWITCH

I believe that in the long run, markets are better than regulators at allocating credit.

—Ben Bernanke, chairman, Federal Reserve

Market discipline in this industry is swift, can be severe, and is more effective in changing lending practices than any potential changes in regulation.

—Doug Duncan, chief economist, Mortgage Bankers Association

MARKETS AND REGULATION—they were not always fighting words. In our parents' and grandparents' time, most of our political leaders and many business leaders believed, with most Americans, that markets and regulation could do more in combination to promote a prosperous and just society than either could do alone. That is still a widespread view in other countries. But in the United States it has become fashionable to depict an irreconcilable conflict between markets (and the private sector) on one side and regulation (and the public sector) on the other.

The rulers of the Soviet world—our longtime archenemies—thought that way, too. But while they set out to manage a vast national economy by edict, our ideologues claim that market forces can solve almost any problem, if we will only do away with those meddlesome regulations. Over the last five or ten years, the home loan business has been something of a test laboratory for that idea, for, as subprime mortgages took off, regulation pretty much collapsed.

JUST ANOTHER "PRIVATE PARTY SITUATION"

Its collapse was only partly a result of laws, court decisions, and other explicit acts of policy. Another big piece of the deregulation story involved the rise of a new set of players—nonbank lenders, brokers, and securities packagers—who were able to exploit the looser regulatory environment and the mood of official complacency to do an end run around the many rules that, in theory, still applied.

With their broker network, the nonbanks were able to operate on a national scale. With Wall Street's backing, they put together a funding and lending mechanism similar to that of the banks and savings and loans they sought to displace. Yet almost all the non-bank lenders chose to be chartered at the state level, generally in states where a single licensed broker was allowed to supervise an officeload of unlicensed colleagues.[1] Since the nonbanks did not hold deposits, they did not have to answer to federal bank examiners either, and they were largely ignored by the various other agencies with mortgage oversight responsibility.

It was these effectively lawless entities—lawless by their own design—that developed the two defining practices of the sub-prime mortgage boom. One was securitization, which enabled the biggest of the nonbanks to lend on a scale rivaling that of big banks. The other was the reliance on brokers, which allowed companies like New Century to market their loans all over the country, incidentally giving them a handy alibi whenever a borrower claimed to have been misled: the broker did it.

It was the nonbanks that came up with the idea of combining an adjustable rate and a teaser rate into an "exploding ARM" and led the way in bringing interest-only loans and balloon payments to the subprime market.[2] Neither type of loan was new; but both, in the past, had been rare and exotic mortgages, reserved for sophisticated borrowers.[3] There was no reason for such loans to be marketed to lower-income borrowers—no reason other than to mislead. But as the profits poured in, mainstream banks began to adopt the same practices, and they, too, got something close to a free pass from the authorities.

By 2005, subprime loans made up some 19 percent of the total mortgage pool, with banks and nonbanks underwriting loans based on teaser rates and making little or no effort to evaluate borrowers' ability to bear the long-term costs.[4] Issuing loans, as many lenders clearly did, based on the value of the property rather than the financial position of the property owner is what predatory mortgage lending is all about; and yet the Federal Reserve— the agency entrusted with monitoring the stability of the nation's banking system—did nothing notable to restrain the practice.[5]

In the Home Ownership and Equity Protection Act of 1994, Congress called on the Fed to act against "unfair or deceptive mortgage lending . . . and abusive refinancing practices."[6] The statute made no distinction between banks and nonbanks, but as Democrat Thomas Dodd, the new chairman of the Senate Banking, Housing and Urban Development Committee, lamented in March 2007, the Fed seemed to take it on itself to decide that non-banks and state-chartered institutions were exempt.[7] Long before the subprime meltdown, members of both parties had pleaded with the Fed to head off what some saw as a coming tidal wave of foreclosure. One exasperated congressman, Republican James Leach of Iowa, denounced the Fed in 2000 for, as he put it, "going AWOL" from its duty to protect homeowners from predatory mortgage lenders.[8]

The Fed eventually responded with a few broadly worded "guidance" documents. But the guidance was not addressed to any bank or lender in particular. A Fed spokesperson explained that the agency *might* have taken some nonpublic action of a more targeted kind. He could not say for sure, he added, because any such action would have been "proprietary and confidential."[9]

To judge by its record, the attitude of the Office of Comptroller of the Currency was equally relaxed. Nearly 1,800 commercial banks across the country fall under OCC supervision; between 2004 and 2006, the agency took a total of just three enforcement actions involving home mortgage loans.[10] Illinois officials thought the OCC might want to know about Dorothy Smith, who had taken out a $36,000 refinancing loan from an OCC-regulated institution, the First Union National Bank (now part of Wachovia). According to her loan documents, Smith had a monthly income of $1,499, though she had actually retired a decade earlier from her job at a Chicago senior citizens home and, at sixty-seven, lived on $540 a month in government benefits.

Smith's loan, including more than $3,300 in fees and closing costs, called on her to make a $31,000 balloon payment in fifteen years, when she would be over eighty. Nevertheless, the OCC dismissed her complaint as "a private party situation regarding the interpretation or enforcement of [a] contract," adding that it could "provide no further assistance."[11]

The Department of Housing and Urban Development sprang to life in 2003, expressing concern about the problem of undisclosed broker fees—yield spread premiums in particular. Yield spread premiums were not new, but the brokers receiving them in the past had been more open about it. Sometimes they served as an alternative to other forms of broker compensation—an alternative that, coming from the lender, allowed cash-strapped borrowers to save money at closing in return for paying a slightly higher interest rate.

In the subprime mortgage business, lenders were offering yield spread premiums to brokers who received substantial commissions as well, and, in some cases, lenders and brokers were working together to keep borrowers in the dark. One big subprime lender, NovaStar, sent out a flier spelling out exactly how a broker could lawfully make a loan "without disclosing YSP!" The message, in effect, was: Send your customers to us, get them to pay a needlessly high interest rate, and we'll pay extra—and you won't have to tell. Whether such a practice could really be lawful (or was an act of fraud by its very nature) became an issue in a class-action lawsuit a few years later. The judge was so startled by NovaStar's position that he asked the company's lawyer if he truly expected to "sell that to the jury" as a nondeceptive practice. "I don't know, Your Honor," the lawyer replied.[12]

Things might not have gotten so far out of hand if HUD had gone ahead in 2003 with a plan to lay down rules calling for more disclosure. But when industry lobbyists objected, the agency backed off. The idea resurfaced four years later. In April 2007 a HUD spokesperson said the agency was again preparing to take action, though he could not yet say how soon.[13]

Across the spectrum of regulators, reactions to the meltdown followed the same general pattern: little outward concern as long as the only clear victims were borrowers; a surge of interest when the damage registered with investors, depositors, and the banking system; words of reassurance once it began to appear that with most of the bad loans safely offloaded and dispersed across the investment community, the banking industry would probably escape another savings and loan–style catastrophe. In terms of "the broader economy and financial markets, the problems in the subprime market" seemed "likely to be contained," said Greenspan's successor, Ben Bernanke.[14]

Bernanke was only the most prominent official of many whose thoughts seemed to shift quickly away from the prospect of millions of people losing their homes. From their public pronouncements after the subprime meltdown, it was often hard to tell the regulators from the regulated. At the Fed and the other oversight agencies, as in the lending industry itself, people in high places seemed more concerned about the banking and credit system than about borrowers. The biggest worry of all, to judge by some of the postmortem comments, was that outsiders looking over the subprime mortgage record might draw broad conclusions about the effects of deregulation on the lending industry. And indeed, that record invited broad conclusions—it was a powerful case study in the disturbing reality (not to be confused with the high-minded theory) of deregulation.

CROSS-COUNTRY BLAME GAME

Deregulation's champions have a lot to say about freedom: the seller's freedom to offer a range of products; the buyer's freedom to choose among them. In the subprime mortgage world, few borrowers got to choose, because they rarely knew they had a choice. But deregulation was often not a liberating experience for people inside the lending industry, either.

Appraisers, for example, found themselves pressured to inflate their valuations. In a 2003 survey, more than half the sampled appraisers reported experiences of that kind.[15] For Richard Hagar, a Seattle-area appraiser, the years of the subprime boom were a period when "every day in my office I received threats, attempts at bribes and was told, 'You make this value,' 'We need it pushed,' 'I'll give you all my business for the rest of the year.' " By refusing to inflate his numbers, Hagar said, he lost most of his clients and saw his staff dwindle from ten appraisers to two. Fraud "crushed my firm."[16]

Impatient with the scruples of Hagar and others, lenders began to pitch assignments to multiple appraisers at once, sending out faxes with cover notes saying, "Can you come in at $750,000?" The first person to respond positively would get the job and the commission, according to Diana Yovino-Young, a Berkeley, California, appraiser. Anyone who came back with a different answer "could lose that client, and that could be 90 percent of their income if they're a one-person shop."[17]

Many appraisers succumbed to the pressure, as evidenced by cases like that of Cheryl Boone in East St. Louis. A single mother of two, her dream of homeownership was undone by a $60,000 mortgage, including nearly $8,000 in points and fees, on a house later found to be worth $15,000 and unlivable.[18]

Deregulation was supposed to stimulate competition. But in the mortgage market, as in the credit card market, the worst players gradually dragged others down to their level. Lenders used to hold onto their own loans and take the hit when one went bad. Now, thanks to securitization, they made their money up front, and, like brokers, kept it even if a borrower defaulted. The big investment banks and other securities packagers kept theirs, too. In all these professions and institutions, integrity became a luxury that many people felt they could not afford.

After the meltdown, burned investors filed lawsuits against subprime mortgage companies, accusing them of reckless loans. Some lenders sought to shift the blame back the other way. William Dallas, founder of the now-bankrupt Ownit, acknowledged that his company's standards had been slack; but he had been asked to loosen them, he said, by Merrill Lynch, which owned a 20 percent stake in his company. Merrill, he told a reporter for the *New York Times,* had leaned on him to do more no-doc loans in order to keep the flow of mortgages coming. The message, according to Dallas, was: "You are leaving money on the table—do more of them." (A Merrill Lynch spokesperson denied that the firm had sent such a message.) Dallas said he had tried to resist—but evidently not for long. "If I can sell it at a profit," he explained, "why should I not do it?"

Brokers adopted a similar line of argument when their practices were questioned.[19] When the Colorado legislature took up a bill intended to establish a fiduciary responsibility on the part of brokers toward borrowers, the president of the state brokers asso-

ciation declared that the proposal reflected a basic misunder-
standing of the profession's role. "The mortgage broker does not
represent the borrower," he said. "We sell access to money."[20]

Initially, the big banks and Wall Street firms had their doubts
about the subprime mortgage business. But they overcame those
doubts when they began to realize how lucrative the business was
getting. In the mid-1990s, Lehman Brothers sent a high-level executive to California to check out one of the early subprime
lenders, First Alliance. The executive reported back that the company operated like a "sweatshop" and employed "high pressure
sales for people who are in a weak state." Lehman nevertheless
concluded (and the executive agreed) that since First Alliance did
not appear to be breaking any laws, it was probably a good bet.
Lehman proceeded to lend First Alliance a cool $500 million while
helping the company sell more than $700 million in mortgage-
backed bonds. Through its dealings with First Alliance and other
lenders, Lehman emerged as the top packager of subprime securities on Wall Street, doing more than $50 billion worth of business
in 2005 and again in 2006.[21]

Some lenders blamed Wall Street; others cited misplaced faith
in credit scores, which, as a spokesperson for HSBC lamented, had
turned out to be "less effective or ineffective" in a time of unusu-
ally low interest rates. A spokesperson for the Fair Isaac Corporation (known as FICO) replied that the company had never
claimed that its scores worked in these circumstances; it was the
lenders who had decided to use them that way.[22]

The end result was a system of institutionalized irresponsibil-
ity. Everyone's fingers got dirty, and yet everyone could point the
finger at someone else. Deregulation had became an escape not

just from a particular set of rules but from rules in general and, by the end, from basic economic accountability. In the name of risk-based lending, an entire industry wound up pushing a product—the exploding ARM—whose key features had nothing to do with risk and everything to do with deception.

HOME TRUTHS

There were many lessons to be drawn, fortunately not all negative. While Washington slept, the states began to awaken. Several enacted reforms directed at practices that seemed abusive in themselves or likely to encourage abuse. Restraints on excessive points and fees, "steering," and no-interest loans with balloon payments were part of a broad antipredatory mortgage-lending bill adopted by the state of North Carolina in 1999. Lenders warned that the proposal would hurt the people it was meant to protect by greatly reducing the availability of credit.[23] It didn't. The clearest consequence was a sharp drop in abusive refinancing loans; North Carolina brokers evidently failed to push them as hard as brokers did elsewhere. Subprime loans for home-buying, meanwhile, increased substantially.[24]

North Carolina, New Mexico, and Iowa were among a group of states that sought to crack down on heavy prepayment penalties. At first, these efforts were checked by uncertainty about whether the states had the authority to act; but after a favorable ruling by the Office of Thrift Supervision in 2003, enforcement intensified, yet again there was no dramatic effect beyond the intended one of giving borrowers an out from loans they had come to regret. (The legal picture was unfortunately clouded once more in April 2007 by a Supreme Court ruling that appeared to reassert the OCC's exclusive jurisdiction in such matters.)[25]

The experiences of the states demonstrated what common sense ought to have told us. Rules do not simply punish people for doing harmful things. They encourage people to do the right thing. Rules help create the sense of fairness and trust that is part of what we are looking for when we go into the marketplace, whether as buyers or sellers.

Credit, like prescription drugs or automobiles or meat, is one of those high-value, high-risk products that need to be regulated. That's not an argument for nit-picking rules or stifling bureaucracy. North Carolina's approach, for example, may not have been perfect. But if similar rules had been in place across the country, the results might have been very different—better for borrowers, for home-buying and economic opportunity, and very probably, in the end, for the lending industry.

6

THE DEBT-FOR-DIPLOMA SYSTEM

SOMETIMES THE STORY in the headlines turns out to be less important than the one we knew—or should have known—all along. Student loans entered the news in March 2007, with the disclosure of what Attorney General Andrew Cuomo of New York State called "an unholy alliance between banks and institutions of higher education."[1] Some of the biggest loan companies, it emerged, had been handing out freebies and favors in order to get colleges and universities to steer business their way.

Pace University and Mercy College, in New York State, were among a number of schools that had agreed to have private lenders operate their financial aid hotlines, so that a student calling in for advice got it, unknowingly, from someone with a stake in the result. Many other schools—too many to name—had charged companies for placement on preferred-lender lists, thus keeping other companies off those lists and making it difficult for students to find out about loans that might have served them better than the ones they got. Financial aid officers at Columbia, Johns Hopkins, and the University of Southern California lost their jobs after it came out that they had personally profited (or had hoped to profit) from undisclosed relationships with lenders.[2] Meanwhile, Congress held hearings and introduced legislation to bring more transparency and accountability to the financial aid process.

It was a situation "filled with the potential for conflicts of interest," as Cuomo rightly said, and yet, at the same time, only the latest plot twist in the continuing scandal of higher education and debt.[3]

WHY WORRY?

Student loans have existed in one form or another for half a century. Until the early 1990s, however, they played a small role in the education of a minority of American college students. States kept tuitions at public universities low, with grant aid typically covering about three-quarters of the expense for a low-income student. The average student could earn enough with a summer job to make up the difference. Not anymore. The states have pulled back, grants have shriveled in value, and loans have become the way most students handle most of the cost of college.

This dramatic shift—from grant-based student aid to what Tamara Draut, in her book *Strapped*, calls a debt-for-diploma system—occurred gradually and without public debate. There's no landmark piece of legislation outlining the new arrangement. Dig to the very bottom of C-SPAN's video archives, and you won't find a formal announcement of America's decision to impose a heaping pile of debt on its young people in the name of helping them get ahead.

Despite its far-reaching consequences, it is a plan without an author. But while no one has claimed credit, many of those now implicated in the system—educators, lenders, congressional leaders, and others—are prepared to defend it. Over a lifetime, they point out, college graduates earn, on average, roughly $1 million more than high school graduates do. Measured against this huge "education premium," we are told, $17,000 in student loan debt (the average that public college students borrow) is hardly worth worrying about.[4] Yet a great many people do worry, and it's not because they can't do the math.

The Project on Student Debt, an organization committed to "keeping college within reach," has carved out a place on its Web site for people to tell their student loan stories. Most of them make painful reading. Troy, for example, is a first-generation college graduate. He and his wife finished school seven years ago with about $60,000 in student loan debt each. Today they owe a combined $200,000, as a result of a long period of forbearance when they were unable to make payments but the interest kept accumulating. They pay about $1,200 a month, according to Troy, with "every penny" now going to interest. "I'm in a position that I feel I will never get out of," he says.

Rebecca borrowed $100,000 to pay for pharmacy school. Her husband borrowed $200,000 for medical school. They pay $3,000 a month. Student loans have become "the main driver of all of our life and career decisions," she says. "Our children will be in and out of college before we pay off our own college education in another twenty-five years or so."

Renee, whose story is told in the book *Strapped*, ran up a student loan bill of $20,000 at a for-profit two-year college. Since then, she has held four different jobs, all administrative in nature, none utilizing her degree in multimedia production. Now working as an office manager, she earns $37,000 a year. Paying off her loans is a remote prospect. She has moved three times since she finished school, and often has trouble making ends meet. She has turned to her mother for help repeatedly. "It's degrading," she says. "I shouldn't have to be doing this. I'm twenty-six years old. I live on my own, I have a full-time job. I shouldn't have to ask my mom to feed me."

Many nonaverage situations go into the reassuring totality of a lifetime average. Some people fail to land the high-paying job that their degrees were intended for. Some discover a preference for a line of work that isn't so remunerative. (A $15,000 or $20,000 debt can loom very large in the finances of a young schoolteacher or nurse or social worker.) Some, along the way to accumulating a respectable lifetime's income, go through tough times when a $200-plus monthly obligation—the payment for the average debt load of recent college grads—can be hard to meet.

And because many high school seniors and their parents have seen—or can imagine—these awkward eventualities, concern about debt begins to shape young people's lives before they have signed a single loan document. More than half of the recent high school graduates questioned in a 2004 survey by the Higher Education Research Institute at UCLA said that money had played a role in their choice of school. More than a quarter of the college students attending what they described as their second-choice college said it was because they "could not afford" their first choice.[5]

Many students try to hold back the tide of debt by working. Three-quarters of all full-time college students have jobs—on campus or off—with nearly half putting in twenty-five hours or more a week, according to U.S. Department of Education figures.[6] Work and college can be a good combination, up to a point. Academic performance, according to some studies, is improved when students work on campus for up to fifteen hours a week. On-campus jobs, which are often designed as work-study arrangements, give students a chance to deepen their connections with other students and faculty. But when students work longer hours at multiple jobs—and when they work off campus as well as on—the formula goes sour. Studying time dwindles (along with time for extracurricular and social activities), grades suffer, and the whole college experience takes on a harsher edge.

In this debt-for-diploma and work-till-you-drop environment, many students get discouraged; fully one-third drop out after the first year. First-generation college students are almost twice as likely as students with college-educated parents to be among the early casualties.[7]

The most common of all cost-reduction strategies—the path followed by more than four hundred thousand college-qualified students from households with incomes of less than $50,000 every year—is to opt for a two-year community college program.[8] The tuition in these programs is significantly lower than it is in four-year programs (though still high enough to produce an average student loan debt of $8,700). But while students often start out with the idea of getting an associate's degree and then transferring to a four-year institution and going for a bachelor's degree, the record shows that only a very small number follow through on that plan.[9]

Community college students are often up against the most

complicated situations—full-time jobs, raising children, working by day, taking classes by night. Five years after entering, only about one in five has gotten as far as an associate's degree.[10] Many leave and never return, and many join the ranks of the estimated one out of five student borrowers who may have set out to get an education at a minimum of expense for themselves and their families, but ended up with the worst of all possible results—debt and no diploma.

A POLICY THAT WORKED

For the two-thirds of college students who borrow to foot the tuition bill, signing up for a loan before stepping onto campus has become part of the college-going ritual. But as their parents and grandparents can attest, it wasn't always this way. Deep inside today's jerry-built financial aid system, you can see the remains of a different structure—one that was purposefully crafted to make college affordable and accessible to any graduating high school student with the smarts and the desire to go.

That earlier structure had builders who *can* be identified. Some, like Franklin Roosevelt and Lyndon Johnson, are well known. One, Harry W. Colmery, deserves far more recognition than he has ever had. Colmery was a leading figure in the Republican Party, a one-time national commander of the American Legion, and the author of the first draft of the Servicemen's Readjustment Act of 1944. The goal of that measure—subsequently nicknamed the GI bill—was to help millions of returning veterans "readjust" to civilian life and provide them with the education, skills, and money to successfully reintegrate into society and the economy. To that end, the GI bill provided grants for tuition, books, and health insurance.

The annual amount available to a veteran in 1948 was $500— enough at the time to pay for all but $25 of a year's tuition at Harvard.[11] On top of that, each veteran got a monthly living-expense stipend of $50—$400 in today's money. As a point of comparison, the average federal grant in 2005 was $2,354—$24,000 short of the tuition and fees at Harvard, and $3,482 short of the public university average.[12]

The GI bill was a spectacular example of what, in a later era, would be called a "big government" program—one enacted, moreover, at a time when the government had already gone deep into debt to pay for the cost of a world war. Yet it produced a reward that few people have ever questioned, paying the country back about $7 for every dollar spent, by some estimates.[13] An estimated 2.3 million veterans took advantage of its higher-education grants; by 1960, the beneficiaries included about half the members of Congress. Through its zero down payment policies and low-interest mortgages, the GI bill helped millions of other veterans and their families buy homes, laying the foundation for the great suburban middle class that symbolized the American dream of widespread prosperity and upward mobility. Not a bad return on a seven-year investment of $91 billion in today's money.[14]

In 1965, the country took another big step forward in its mission of making college affordable for most young people, not just the privileged few. That year, Congress passed the Higher Education Act, extending GI bill–style benefits to nonveterans and creating the grants and loans on which today's system is largely based. The goal, President Lyndon Johnson said when he signed the bill, was to ensure that "a high school senior anywhere in this great land of ours can apply to any college or any university in any of the fifty states and not be turned away because his family is poor."

As a result of this landmark legislation, countless young Americans became the first in their families to attend college; the number of low-income college students nearly doubled between 1965 and 1971.[15] For poor kids, grants were generous enough to cover the cost of going to school. For the middle class, tuition at public universities remained low enough to allow most students to pay the price of admission with a part-time job and some help from Mom and Dad.

In 1972, Congress reaffirmed its commitment to the Higher Education Act—both the goal and the means—by creating what came to be known as Pell grants, in honor of their Senate champion, Claiborne Pell of Rhode Island. Throughout the 1970s, low-income students continued to close in on the enrollment rates of their wealthier contemporaries. The United States was on the way to achieving what Richard Nixon—a Republican president, echoing the words of his Democratic predecessor—called "the great American goal" of a society in which "no qualified student who wants to go to college should be barred by lack of money."[16]

Average tuition in the late 1970s for a four-year public college was just over $2,192, in 2006 dollars.[17] Add in room and board, and the total cost was still under $6,900. For those with more substantial means, the tuition at a private college was in the $9,000 neighborhood; the inflation-adjusted total, with room and board included, came to $14,000. To put that into perspective, the cost of attending a private university in 1976 was only slightly higher than the cost of attending a public university today. Borrowing your way through college wasn't the norm, because it wasn't necessary.

TRAGEDY OF NEGLECT

Two-thirds of all financial aid used to come from grants. Now two-thirds comes from loans. What happened? Mainly, it is a story of what did not happen. Over a span of thirty years, elected officials failed to maintain adequate funding for Pell grants, decimating their purchasing power in the wake of rising costs and surging enrollments. Today's debt-for-diploma system—dominated, shaped, and promoted by the profit interests of lenders—came about without any formal repudiation or public debate of the grant aid and low-cost state tuition of our parents' and grandparents' time. American leaders simply let crucial elements of the old structure decay through neglect.

In the states, elected officials cut back on funding for public colleges and universities, resulting in steeply rising tuitions. In per-pupil terms, state-level spending on higher education has fallen to a twenty-five-year low, even as government officials and corporate leaders keep pounding out the message of a college degree as the key to a successful future.[18] In one generation, tuition at public universities has risen 122 percent, from $2,628 in 1986–1987 to $5,836 in 2006–2007 (in 2006 dollars).[19] In the last five years alone, tuition and fees at public universities have gone up 40 percent, taking inflation into account.[20]

The federal government, for its part, beat a long retreat from the commitment that, in the 1970s, enabled Pell grants to cover

75 percent of the cost of going to college for most low- and moderate-income students. The maximum award today covers about one-third the average expense of tuition and fees at a four-year private college, and only 22 percent of all grant recipients actually get the maximum.[21] The average award in 2006 was $2,354, which came to less than half the public university average.[22] In September 2007, Congress passed a bill to increase the maximum Pell grant from its current level of $4,310 to $5,400 in 2012.[23]

Just as grant funding was drying up, states were moving resources from need-based to so-called merit-based aid programs. Between 1994 and 2004, spending by the states on need-based scholarships for undergraduates increased by 95 percent, while spending on merit-based aid increased by 350 percent. The proportion of state grants awarded on the basis of merit rather than need rose from 13 percent to 27 percent during this period.[24] Meanwhile, universities themselves—public as well as private— became caught up in a costly competition for a small pool of top students, which led them to dispense an increasingly large share of aid dollars to those who could afford the cost of college without any aid. In 1995, for example, the average student from a family with an income below $20,000 received $836 in institutional grant aid, while the average student from a family earning $100,000 or more received $239 in grant aid. In 2003, the average award to low-income students had increased 50 percent, to $1,251, while the average award to students from families earning above $100,000 had grown 227 percent, to $781.[25]

A similar mind-set led to an increased reliance on the tax code to soften the cost crunch for middle- and even high-income households. By 2003, 43 percent of all education tax credits and 70 percent of the benefits of federal tuition tax deductions went to families with annual incomes of more than $50,000.[26] Other families—those without the resources to save for their children's college educations or to take advantage of special tax incentives—were forced to borrow instead.

This slow backward drift has left a generation of young Americans billions of dollars in debt. It has surely cost the nation far more in lost potential, as increasing numbers of students buckle under the financial pressure and more and more potential students look at today's skyrocketing tuitions and exploding loans and conclude that the system was not meant for them.

Indeed, under the current arrangements, the less money you and your family have at the start, the more, as a rule, you'll owe in the end. Among Pell grant recipients who earned their degrees in 2004, 88.5 percent had student loans, compared to just over half of non-Pell recipients.[27] Pell grant recipients also carried 12 percent higher debt—a student loan total, on average, of $20,735, versus $18,420 for non-Pell recipients. The sting of high college prices and dwindling grant aid has hit those least able to absorb the shock.

As a result, the gains made during the 1970s in expanding access to college have begun to erode. In fact, the gap in college enrollment between white students, on the one hand, and black and Hispanic students, on the other, has actually widened over the last thirty years, as has the college enrollment gap by socio-economic status.[28] Today, the highest-performing students from low-income families enroll in college at the same rate as the lowest-performing students from high-income families. To put it more bluntly, the smartest poor kids attend college at the same rate as the dumbest rich kids.[29]

TODAY'S STUDENTS, TOMORROW'S DEBTORS

Once you're on the hook, there's no easy escape from student loans. The federal government can be a persistent creditor, and it has collection methods all its own—seizing a tax refund, for example, or tapping into a stream of benefit checks.[30] Bankruptcy? Think again. Student loans, unlike other forms of credit, cannot be discharged that way. There's no statute of limitations, either.[31] About 9 percent of Americans between the ages of fifty-five and sixty-four have student loan debt (the average balance is $17,498). Sandra, at fifty-nine, is one of them. Another contributor to the Project on Student Debt story bank, she writes: "I am not in a high-paying field. I teach at a university and my students are working professionals who work with young children with disabilities." She expects to be making payments until 2012. "I will not fully pay this loan," she says, "until I am almost old enough to receive Social Security."

The average graduate leaves college today with $19,300 in student loan debt (up from $9,250 a little over a decade ago).[32] Despite the hardships, most young adults believe that the personal growth and career opportunities of a college degree make the debt worthwhile. They wish they could have borrowed less, but, by and large, they wouldn't trade their degree for a debt-free existence. Most are doing their best to cope with the payment burden.

Even so, debt often has a powerful effect on people's lives. It influences decisions about where to live, what job to take, and even when to get married. Surveys conducted by the Nellie Mae Corporation between 1987 and 2002 provide a revealing snapshot of the attitudes and experiences of recent graduates. In the Nellie Mae surveys, the great majority of graduates said that their career plans had not been affected by student loans. But the number who said the opposite increased from one poll to the next, as debt levels and monthly payment bills went up. Since 2002, of course, they have continued to go up—the average monthly payment rising from $180 to $220, or, as a share of income, from 10 percent to about 16 percent.[33]

A recent survey of Princeton University graduates may shed more light on the debt-career connection. These graduates had no student loans to pay off, thanks to Princeton's trailblazing decision, in 2001, to replace all student loans with grants. University officials were not thinking about postcollege careers when they adopted that plan; the idea was simply to reduce the debt-work burden for lower- and middle-income students, in the hope of attracting more of them. But by 2005, when the university surveyed its first class of debt-free graduates, two-thirds cited the new financial aid policy as an important factor in their career plans. A number said it had allowed them to consider the possibility of becoming a teacher or working for a nonprofit.[34]

Law school provides more dramatic evidence of the way debt can narrow the range of career options. Most law students take out loans; many finish with $100,000 or more in total debt. According to a recent survey by the National Association for Law Placement, student loans kept nearly two-thirds of all law student respondents from even considering a public service career.[35]

In the Nellie Mae surveys, graduates were asked about the difficulty of making loan payments. The obligation felt most burdensome, according to the surveys, to the most recent graduates—a logical finding, since that's when loan payments loom largest in proportion to income, as a rule. Yet, surprisingly, those who have been making loan payments for three years or more begin to feel *more* burdened, not less. The survey doesn't ask why—maybe because after three years people begin to realize that the debt will hang over them longer than they first suspected; or maybe because, by then, they're more likely to have other financial obligations such as car payments or rent in addition to their student loans.

The guaranteed-loan program limits the annual amount that any one student can borrow.[36] The top figure for a first-year student is $2,625; for a second-year student, $3,500; for a third- or fourth-year student, $5,500. Those maximums were ample when loans played a supplementary role in a grant-centered system. Now, with average tuition and fees approaching $13,000 at public universities, students are coming up short even when they borrow right on up to the limit.

As the level of debt has increased, so has the cost of debt, because of the growing proportion of student loans being issued by private lenders outside the federal rules. Federal loans carry fixed interest rates, currently capped at 6.8 percent. With private loans, interest is unregulated and "risk-based lending" enters the picture, though Congress passed legislation in September 2007 that will gradually reduce the interest rate on new subsidized loans to 3.4 percent in 2011. Several lenders have already come out with loans supposedly designed for students and families with poor credit histories—loans typically carrying interest rates in the 16 to 18 percent neighborhood, according to Bankrate.com. One company, Loan to Learn, has interest rates reaching as high as 16 percent *on top of* a 10 percent up-front fee![37]

There are other differences. The federal program includes deferred-payment options for borrowers who face economic hardship; private loans don't have any safety net. But with the cost of college far outstripping even the level of debt that the government is prepared to guarantee (by the 2006 school year, room, board, and tuition and fees at public universities averaged $12,796), many students don't see any choice. Private loans were a drop in the financial aid bucket as recently as a decade ago; by 2006, they had increased fourteenfold, from $1.2 billion to $17 billion.[38]

PRIVATE PROFIT WITH PUBLIC SUPPORT

Smaller grants; bigger loans; expensive private loans on top of low-interest public loans; still more expensive loans for those least able to pay—the debt-for-diploma system has been a disaster for young adults and for students and would-be students. But it has been very good for the lending industry, and no company has gained more from the system—or done more to shape and protect it—than the one that began life as the Student Loan Marketing Association, now known as Sallie Mae.

Sallie Mae was set up in 1972 as a federally chartered corporation to support the Federal Family Education Loan Program (FFELP), the loan arm of the Higher Education Act of 1965. Although the loans issued under that program came from private lenders, they were subject to interest rate caps and other rules. The government, in exchange, agreed to be the repayer of last resort; participating lenders also received subsidies that, by a complicated formula (updated every year), were designed to give them a set rate of return. Sallie Mae's role was to buy and service loans—

and securitize them—so that lenders would have more money to give out.

Although student loans were a small part of the financial aid stream at first, demand increased rapidly with the growing ranks of college students. It increased even more rapidly in the 1980s and 1990s as tuitions soared, grants failed to keep up, and debt took up the slack, adding up to a very nice business for the lenders and for Sallie Mae as well.

It was at this point in the story—in 1997, precisely—that Sallie Mae, under its then-CEO Albert L. Lord, renounced its federal charter and mandate, transformed itself into a publicly traded corporation, and entered the loan-dispensing business in its own right. Lord and his associates were heirs to an old tradition of American business leaders: preaching the wonders of the market and the superior efficiency of the private sector while dipping heavily into the public trough. Their strategy was to use Sallie Mae's privileged position and enormous financial heft (achieved through its federal mandate) to become the dominant company in the guaranteed-loan business, where the risk is essentially all covered by the taxpayers, and then in the even more profitable growth market of wholly private, unregulated student loans.

They had it nicely figured. Today, according to Sallie Mae's Web site, it owns or manages student loans for almost 10 million Americans and employs some twelve thousand people. In addition to being the biggest player in the guaranteed-loan market, Sallie Mae has captured about 40 percent of the market for private student loans.[39]

How much are those markets worth? Enough to enable Sallie

Mae's former CEO (now board chairman) to personally rack up $228 million in stock options and other compensation. Enough to give this government-created and government-subsidized entity a continual spot on the Fortune 500. Enough, in April 2007, to inspire a syndicate of private equity funds and banks—including two of the other leading players in the student loan business, Bank of America and JPMorgan Chase—to put together a $25 billion offer to take Sallie Mae private, with its top executives set to realize hundreds of millions in payouts for themselves.

Only a few weeks earlier, Sallie Mae had reached a $2 million settlement with the New York State attorney general's office. Along with a number of other lenders, Sallie Mae had agreed to refrain from a list of anticompetitive practices. Meanwhile, questions were being raised about Lord's sale of four hundred thousand shares of Sallie Mae stock. The sales had taken place a few days before the Bush administration issued a budget proposal calling for cutbacks in loan subsidies—and a few days *after* a meeting between Sallie Mae officials and administration officials. Through his deft timing, Lord had probably saved about $1.4 million, according to the *Washington Post* story that revealed the sequence of events. (A Sallie Mae spokesperson said that the timing was coincidental, and the scope of the proposed cutbacks unanticipated.)

The casual observer might have taken all these stories as signs of fundamental change in the student loan world. Insiders, as the Sallie Mae takeover bid made clear, knew better. The smart money was still on the lenders, not the students.

WHO'S IN CHARGE HERE?

It was the complaints of an upstart lender, MyRichUncle, that set off the student loan probe. That company's two young founders, Raza Khan and Vishal Garg, claimed that their efforts to offer students a better deal had been frustrated by a conspiracy of the heavyweight lenders. Their charges were abundantly confirmed by the ensuing investigation. But the deeper scandal—the debt-for-diploma system, with its ever-increasing reliance on loans, in the first place, and unregulated private loans, in the second place—remained untouched.

The investigation's focus was on the lending industry's influence with college officials. The real story was—and is—the industry's influence with elected officials. College students might save a little money if they had a few more loan companies to choose from. But what they really need is a show of courage and integrity from the country's leaders. That is the only development that could make a real difference in the student loan story. And it is the only thing that the big lenders are really scared of.

Most of the loans issued under the federal program are the guaranteed kind that the industry thrives on—most, but not all. There is an alternative. It's called direct lending. The William D. Ford Federal Direct Loan program, launched nationally in 1993, was an attempt to find out whether costs could be reduced with the government issuing the loans itself. They were reduced—dramatically. Unlike federally guaranteed student loans, which cost taxpayers 7 cents on every dollar in subsidies to private student lenders, the Direct Loan program costs less than 4 cents per dollar lent.[40]

Proponents in Congress and the Clinton administration originally hoped to switch all federal loans from the guaranteed program to the direct program. By doing so, the Congressional Budget Office has estimated, the federal government could save $12 billion over ten years as a result of lower subsidies and administrative expenses.[41] Because of opposition from Republicans and the student loan industry, however, a compromise was reached. Instead of replacing FFELP, the Direct Loan program would compete with it—but it would not be allowed to market its loans the way Sallie Mae and other student lenders do. When the Republicans retook control of Congress in 1994, they passed a law prohibiting the Education Department from encouraging or requiring colleges to participate in the Direct Loan program. Thoroughly hamstrung, the program has been losing ground for the past decade; the number of participating schools, never higher than 30 percent, is now down to 25 percent.[42]

This is turf that Sallie Mae and others will defend with all their might. With the election of 2006 and the shift of party control on Capitol Hill (and committee leadership positions going to House and Senate members who had been critical of the subsidies in the past), industry leaders see a fresh threat to their near-monopoly grip on federal financial aid. In a remarkable eighteen-page internal strategy memo—obtained and released by the House Education Committee in May 2007—Sallie Mae's lobbyists emphasized the need to "grow the FFELP Coalition within the Democratic party" and "arm Congressional Republicans and Administration to combat irresponsible proposals."[43]

The industry's number one goal for 2007 and 2008, according to the memo, is to "protect FFELP economics"—in other words, to protect the gravy train of subsidies that lenders receive on federal student loans. If history is any guide, they will protect it well. While Congress finally acted to increase the maximum Pell grant by a few hundred dollars—by trimming subsidies from FFELP—it still isn't enough to allow low-income students to pay for college without going into massive debt, and it certainly isn't enough to shift the center of gravity of the system. Borrowing will continue to be the lifeblood of that system, with lenders reaping profits and young people living in the red.

7

STICKING IT TO THE SICK

PEGGIE SHERRY was running cancer camps for children when she learned about her own breast cancer. She got the diagnosis in November 2002. At the time, Peggie and her husband, Glen, had a joint income of $140,000 a year, placing them comfortably in the top 10 percent of American families. They owned a four-bedroom house in a gated community of north Tampa, Florida. They had a savings account and health insurance. In other words, they had checked off just about every possible box on the scorecard of financial responsibility. Nevertheless, Peggie's illness became a financial as well as a physical calamity.

Over a span of two years, she went through six surgeries, countless tests and doctor visits, and what felt like an unending series of battles over bills and reimbursement. As Peggie navigated the dizzying gaps in her insurance coverage and dealt with a succession of health care providers and bill collectors, the family savings disappeared and the debts mounted. By the time her cancer had been eradicated, Peggie and Glen owed $40,000—$10,000 of it on credit cards—and they were struggling to hold onto their

house because Glen had fallen five months behind on the mortgage payments without telling her.[1]

A solidly upper-middle-class family pushed to the brink of financial ruin by illness—it's not the popular perception of debt in
America, but it's part of a growing reality. We're spending more on
health care as a society—health care costs account for 16 percent
of gross domestic product, up from 13.8 percent as recently as
2000—and handing larger bills to sick people and their families
directly.[2] As a result, only the richest Americans stand more than a
major illness away from being hit with medical bills far beyond
any amount they could reasonably afford.

FRAGMENTED, POROUS, AND RISKY

Health insurance in the United States is a divided responsibility.
One part of the job goes to the private sector, and another part to
the public sector—leaving aside, for the moment, the part that
falls through the cracks. We look to employers, by and large, to
cover full-time workers and their dependents, while government
(through Medicare, Medicaid, and the State Children's Health Insurance Program) takes responsibility for insuring the elderly, the
disabled, and low-income children as well as some parents.

Health insurance has two purposes: to protect people from expensive and unpredictable medical costs and to ensure access to a
network of providers. To achieve these results, an insurance system needs to be universal, seamless, and comprehensive. Ours
meets none of these requirements.

It is neither seamless nor universal because it was designed for a
different era. It was designed, to be precise, for World War II, when

employers were competing for a diminished labor supply. With paychecks capped by wartime wage-and-price controls, companies began offering health insurance as an extra lure. After the war, rapid advances in medicine increased the cost of health care, and the need for it, and health insurance continued to be seen as a valuable fringe benefit. By the 1950s, employer-sponsored health insurance had become a tax-free benefit, thanks to an Internal Revenue Service ruling that greatly accelerated the growth of the employment-based system.[3]

That system worked fairly well in the manufacturing-based economy of the postwar era. With spouses and children piggybacking on the benefits of employees, company health plans provided stable coverage for a substantial part of the population. In the large corporations where a great many Americans worked, these plans served to bring people of widely varying health statuses into a common risk pool, allowing management to take a relaxed view of any particular employee's medical bills.

Since the late 1970s, the defects of our system have been highlighted and magnified by soaring health care costs and general economic turbulence. The biggest problem is the most obvious: the large and growing number of Americans with no coverage at all. Even before the uninsured became an issue, they were numerous, and they included some of the same groups—agricultural and domestic workers, for example—cruelly neglected by Social Security and the other safety net programs of the pre–civil rights era. In more recent decades, the ranks of the uninsured have shot up from 31 million in 1987 to 47 million in 2006.[4] Even that figure ignores the tens of millions of Americans who churn in and out of the system every year, getting stuck with the cost of any health care problem that happens to arise between coverage periods. (Twenty-eight percent of all adults between the ages of nineteen and sixty-four went without insurance at some point in 2005, according to a study by the Commonwealth Fund.)[5] Most workers still have employment-based coverage, but the system is unraveling. Today's typical worker has been with an employer for only four years; transitions from one insurance plan to another, or periods of "going bare," have become common.[6] In other words, our health insurance delivery system was set up for an economy that scarcely resembles the one we live and work in.

If you're uninsured, you pay the whole bill, and it's likely to be a bigger bill *because* you're uninsured. (More about that later.) Nevertheless, if you're concerned about being dragged deep into debt by a health emergency, insurance is no longer any guarantee that you won't be. Nowadays, even so-called good insurance plans can be riddled with gaps: excluded medications, procedures, and equipment; uncovered services for children with special needs; and higher rates of cost sharing for out-of-network providers, in addition to multiple deductibles.[7] More than a fifth of workers are in insurance plans without an out-of-pocket maximum, so when illness strikes and unreimbursed costs mount, there is no limit on how high they can go before the insurer assumes them.[8] About half of workers have plans with a lifetime benefit maximum, so those with rare but exceedingly costly medical expenses can actually hit a cap on the expenses their insurer will cover, leaving them to pay the rest. (Lifetime benefit maximums are usually in the $1 to $2 million dollar range.)[9]

Of the estimated 29 million Americans with medical debt of one kind or another, more than two-thirds had insurance when they fell into that predicament.[10] Plainly, health insurance in the United States today is failing to meet its purpose. Yet, rather than trying to plug the gaps, policymakers have been encouraging insurance practices that expose patients to higher and higher costs.

A BLUNT INSTRUMENT

A brief detour through "free market" economic ideology may help explain why. Conservative policymakers like to talk about the systemic waste created by a system of third-party payment. Traditional health insurance, they argue, poses a "moral hazard" to society by shielding consumers from the cost of their health care consumption.[11] To solve the problem, they would shift some of the expense back to individuals, compensating them with tax-favored or subsidized health savings accounts and letting the money be rolled over from year to year. By constructing a system that forces people to pay more of the cost out of their own pockets (the thinking goes), we can get Americans to shop around, negotiate better prices with their physicians, and think twice before they agree to unnecessary (or unnecessarily expensive) care.

Even as a theoretical proposition, there are problems with this model: vulnerable patients are generally in no state to bargain with their doctors, nor do most people have the leverage to whittle prices down. According to the best research we have (a landmark study by RAND conducted, unfortunately, back in the 1970s), higher out-of-pocket costs for patients do lead to lower utilization of health services, but that applies to needed as well as unneeded services, and patients aren't well positioned to make the distinction.[12] In other words, cost sharing turns out to be a very blunt instrument of cost control. Nevertheless, inspired by conservative philosophy and rhetoric, Congress set out on this path in 2003 by authorizing tax benefits for Health Savings Accounts (HSAs) linked to high-deductible insurance plans.

While the "moral hazard" analysis may apply to some situations—excessive drinking when people are being served at an open bar, for example—health care is not like other products and services. Many people, left to their own devices, would prefer less of it, not more; most people, recognizing the limitations of their own knowledge, try to find a physician they trust, and then do their best to follow his or her advice. When consumers overpurchase, it is often because doctors and hospitals (whose profits depend on the number and complexity of services they deliver) have oversold. Policymakers might do well to worry less about patient incentives and more about provider incentives or even insurer incentives, for, under today's arrangements, insurers are economically motivated to pay for as little health care as possible.

They go about it in two ways. The first approach is to sort people by risk and refuse to cover the sickest and most vulnerable. In 2006, California insurers rejected about 12 percent of all applicants for individual coverage and about 30 percent of those over the age of fifty-eight.[13] The disqualifying factors ranged, according to reporter Amy Girion of the *Los Angeles Times,* from "the catastrophic to the common"—from "cancer, epilepsy and AIDS," to "breast implants, ear infections, varicose veins and sleep apnea." One young woman was turned down because, in Girion's words, "she had seen a psychologist for three months after breaking up with a boyfriend"; another was rejected because of a past episode of jock itch, "successfully treated with cream."[14]

In most states, individuals without access to employer-sponsored coverage face this sort of risk-sorting when they shop for insurance in the private market, and their premiums—assuming they find an insurer willing to cover them—are determined in large part by their health status. Employment-based coverage is different in one crucial way: your eligibility will not depend, as a rule, on your health. But in recent years, insurers and employers have taken steps to make company plans less reliable and comprehensive. The net effect is that while employers still pay much of the cost of job-based coverage, the financial burden on workers is substantial. Between 2000 and 2006, insurance premiums increased by 73.8 percent, and with incomes failing to keep up, insurance costs now take a much bigger bite out of Americans' pockets.[15]

While public debate continues to focus on the uninsured, health policy experts argue that we should be paying more attention to the underinsured. By some estimates, they include more than 15 million Americans, and their numbers, too, are growing rapidly. In 2001, about 28 percent of all low-income people with private insurance and chronic health conditions were underinsured, according to one widely used set of criteria; just two years later, the proportion was 42 percent.[16] For the chronically ill, underinsurance can mean a succession of costs incurred and not adequately reimbursed. For healthier people, it can be a nasty surprise—a state of affairs that doesn't become fully apparent until illness strikes.

Peggie Sherry had not given much thought to the scope of her insurance plan when she first signed up for it. Cancer became her education in all the things her insurance didn't quite cover. Because she worked for a small organization, her policy had been purchased in the nongroup market. That meant that before her insurance kicked in each year, Peggie had to meet a $2,500 deductible. Even then, she remained responsible for 20 percent of the costs—40 percent if she went out of network, and, as she and others have found, it is possible to slip out of network even when you make every reasonable effort to stay in. Peggie had chosen a network hospital, for example, but once that decision was behind her, she did not think to verify the network tie of every doctor who worked there. When she needed anesthesia, she learned that none of the available anesthesiologists in that hospital happened to be in her network—a discovery that prompted her to ask if she was supposed to "walk across the street to the guy in my plan and then come back?"[17] It was experiences like this that she had in mind when, in a letter to her insurance company, she wrote: "You are worse than the cancer. I can cut out the cancer but I have to work with you."[18]

BILKING THE UNINSURED

There are as many myths about the uninsured as there are about the insured. Between Medicare (the federal program that covers the elderly) and Medicaid (the federal and state program designed to protect the poor), most Americans assume that we have a system of reliable protection for those in greatest need. We don't. Although it's not widely known, the eligibility criteria for Medicaid leave about 36 percent of the poor unprotected; this is twice the overall uninsured rate in the nonelderly population (18 percent). The lower you go down the income ladder, in fact, the higher the proportion of uninsured. Two-thirds of the uninsured are either poor or near-poor, although the vast majority (80 percent) are in working families (69 percent of the uninsured have at least one full-time worker in the family). Correlations with race and ethnicity are also striking: while about 13 percent of whites lacked insurance in 2005, the figure was 19 percent for Asians, 21 percent for blacks, and 34 percent for Latinos.[19]

According to another popular belief—also comforting, also unfortunately mistaken—the uninsured at least have the fallback option of being treated for free at a public hospital. In fact, uninsured patients are routinely billed for services they receive at public and private hospitals alike, and unlike insurers, who get a negotiated discount, they are expected to pay the sticker price.

This two-tiered pricing system was a pervasive but fairly uncontroversial practice until 2003, when it became the subject of a disturbing series of articles in the *Wall Street Journal.* In one story, reporter Lucette Lagnado wrote about nonprofit hospitals pursuing "body attachments" (a fancy name for arrests) of medical debtors who had failed to show up for their court hearings; this was happening, Lagnado noted, even though such hospitals generally receive money from the federal government for uncompensated care. Marlin Bushman, an Illinois truck driver, was briefly jailed over $579 in outstanding hospital charges for diabetes treatment. Kara Atteberry, a twenty-six-year-old single mother, suffered the same fate over a $1,678 debt related to a miscarriage.[20]

Paul Shipman, an uninsured Virginia furniture salesman, suffered a heart attack and, though hospitalized for less than twenty-four hours, ran up an astonishing $37,000 in charges. Going over Shipman's bill, Lagnado compared it, item by item, with the amounts that Virginia Medicaid would have paid. Among other peculiarities, Lagando noted a $7,560 charge for a stent that a hospital could have obtained from the manufacturer for less than half that, and a $39.15 bill for a small volume of saline solution that could have been bought at a pharmacy for $15 a liter. Even the ambulance ride, at $1,000, cost more than five times the Medicaid-approved figure.[21] Overall, Shipman had been charged more than four times what Medicaid would have reimbursed.

The *Wall Street Journal* articles sparked a firestorm of criticism. The U.S. Department of Health and Human Services and the American Hospital Association responded with new billing and collection guidelines.[22] The House Committee on Energy and Commerce held hearings. David Scruggs, the plaintiff's attorney known for his landmark litigation against the tobacco industry, filed a class-action lawsuit against hospital systems across the country. When the federal courts threw out his cases, Scruggs went into state courts with the same complaints. (Some of these lawsuits have been settled; others are still pending.)[23] Responding to the media attention and political pressure, California, Colorado, Connecticut, Illinois, Minnesota, New York, and Wisconsin passed laws cracking down on egregious billing and collection practices.[24]

As a result, some hospitals now offer uninsured patients the same discounts as insurers, and some provide extra financial help for their lowest-income patients. But the basic financial equation has not changed: health care providers, including most hospitals, give the insured (and insurers) the best deal and seek to compensate by charging others more and accelerating their efforts to collect. Lately, though, providers have been gravitating toward a new form of "financial assistance"—one that holds the promise of protecting them from getting stuck with the bill or with the bad publicity.

PAYING WITH PLASTIC

Donna, a Massachusetts mother whose daughter, Grace, has cerebral palsy, found her family $30,000 in debt despite having health insurance. Grace's condition required ongoing, costly treatments and durable medical equipment, and insurance didn't always cover the expense. To give Grace the attention she needed, Donna cut back to a part-time job, using credit cards to pay the medical bills. She and her husband declared bankruptcy in 2003.[25]

The use of credit cards to pay for health care has risen dramatically in recent years.[26] And it's not because millions of people spontaneously began offering their cards when they checked into the hospital or showed up at the doctor's office. It's because health care providers are now far more insistent on up-front collection when they're dealing with copays, deductibles, and the growing number of "self-pay" patients, as they have come to be known. And the number one strategy is to get credit card information before giving treatment.[27]

In 2005, Demos and the Center for Responsible Lending surveyed some 1,150 low- and middle-income households with credit card debt. Nearly a third said they had used credit cards to pay medical expenses.[28] Those households were also notable for having substantially higher levels of credit card debt—an average of $11,623 versus $7,964 for households without medical debt. Forty-four percent of medically indebted families had credit card debt of more than $10,000.[29]

When medical bills go onto credit cards, health problems become tangled up with all the problems of credit cards—the unpredictable interest rates and the maze of terms, conditions, and fees.[30] Even in the best of times, it can be difficult to avoid the myriad mistakes that are the credit card industry's bread and butter. Illness only increases the odds of error. As anyone who has ever had a loved one in the hospital can attest, paying bills late is par for the course in such circumstances, so the last thing sick people need is a form of financing in which a day's (or even an hour's) delay can bring a dramatic increase in borrowing costs. And yet this is exactly what has happened to millions of Americans.

In suburban Boston, Lauren and Jefferson Riordan accumulated more than $3,000 in medical and dental expenses on their credit cards, partly because Lauren's medical insurance had a $650 deductible for prescriptions. (Once she could get drugs for a $5 copayment, but that provision was eliminated years ago.) Lauren Riordan fell into the habit of shifting medical debt from card to card, watching the mail for zero percent interest rate offers and transferring balances—it had all became a matter of course to her. "You need a prescription because you have an infection or something," she told a *Boston Globe* reporter, "and you just put it on your credit card."[31] Sadly, a great many other Americans have also begun to think that way.

DOWNHILL SLIDE

A temp worker—young, healthy, and uninsured—gets into a serious car accident. A sales clerk with a high-deductible insurance plan has a complicated pregnancy. A teacher has a chronically ill child.

Medical debt can take many forms. When health care expenses go onto a credit card, they become indistinguishable from other categories of "consumer debt." The problem is hard to define and hard to measure; partly for that reason, the issue has been very nearly invisible to policymakers. Over the past several years, however, research has begun to shed light on the magnitude of America's medical-debt problem, and on some of the ways in which it reverberates through people's lives.

Like student loans and other college-related debt, medical debt can damage people's credit ratings, complicating their efforts to save money or buy a home. Those who already own houses often have difficulty keeping up with their mortgage payments—a problem that may be aggravated by the decision to take out a refinancing loan in order to deal with medical or credit card debt. According to a study conducted by the Access Project, more than a quarter of those with medical debt had experienced such difficulties.[32] Peggie Sherry was able to save her home and her credit. But the way she did it is hardly a method she could recommend. While she was going through her cancer nightmare, both her parents died, leaving her an inheritance that allowed her to pay her bills.

Through the channel of debt, medical problems can lead to problems in other realms of life. They can also turn around and become a cause of illness (or a contributing factor) in their own right. That potential is plain when the medically indebted decide to forgo further treatment rather than add to their debts. Evidence suggests that this may be a widespread tendency. One study looked at people with medical debt who eventually filed for bankruptcy; in the two years before doing so, 60 percent of those surveyed went without some needed doctor or dental visits, while almost half did not fill prescriptions.[33]

Another study, conducted by the Kaiser Family Foundation, showed that patients with medical debt *and* insurance were more than five times as likely as their unindebted counterparts to delay care, more than twice as likely to leave needed drug prescriptions unfilled, and more than three times as likely to skip recommended treatments and tests. If the current trend toward greater patient cost-sharing continues, "more low- and middle-income families with private insurance, particularly if they are less healthy, will not have the same access to care as others with private coverage who have higher incomes," the study's authors observe.[34] To put it another way, we have a health care system that is designed to discourage a growing number of sick people from seeing doctors.

But while lack of treatment can make sick people sicker, the worry and stress of debt hold the same potential. The connection between stress and sickness—folk wisdom for centuries—has, in our own time, been repeatedly validated by mainstream research. In one recent study, researchers found significant health deterioration in a group of British civil servants after they learned of a plan to privatize their department—but before they lost their jobs.[35] When physicians are advising patients who have suffered heart attacks or traumatic surgery, they often do not hesitate to talk about the importance of avoiding stressful situations. By the same logic, the medical profession ought to be up in arms about public and private policies that make illness an occasion for taking on debt and financial anxiety. So far, though, there has been no outcry. Instead, the thinking of many in the health care field seems to be moving in the opposite direction.

In the past few years, health care providers big and small have teamed up with lenders to market a brand-new product: the medical credit card. The concept means different things to different providers. Some cards are meant to serve the patients of a particular hospital. Some are designed, more generally, for the growing number of Americans whose high-deductible plans leave them with substantial uncovered expenses. Some cards carry an aura of charity and good works. Some are fairly standard credit cards, with a health care company getting a piece of the action. And sometimes it's hard to tell which is which. Citibank's Citi Health Card, for example—offered to patients through participating health care providers—has monthly payments as low as $10 with a zero-interest provision for patients who pay down their medical debt quickly through higher monthly payments. But if you don't do that, eventually you'll find yourself paying more than 20 percent in annual interest on the balance.[36]

One big thing all such cards have in common: they shift the bill-collecting responsibility from the provider to the card issuer.[37] Nina Heck, a counseling officer at the Consumer Credit Counseling Service of Maryland and Delaware, works with elderly people who are struggling to pay for prescriptions. To Heck, medical credit cards are "just a quick way to pay that bill and get out of the office."[38]

Medical credit cards are a new phenomenon, and we don't yet know where they will lead. Even so, it is not too soon to consider the parallels with higher education. If the health care industry follows the path of the student loan industry, we can expect to see lenders paying off hospitals and other providers to steer people their way, and we can expect to hear stories of patients making borrowing decisions under pressure and not quite knowing whether they're getting the best deal or where the advice is really coming from. Eventually, those engaged in the effort to reform the dysfunctional U.S. health system can look forward to the prospect of battling a powerful new alliance of providers and lenders united in their determination to keep things the way they are.

8

THE McSHARKS

IN THE BEGINNING, there was the pawnshop. What may be the oldest of all lending institutions goes back, if not to the Garden of Eden, a long way. The basic business model was already established in China two or three thousand years ago: you borrow some money; you leave some collateral; you lose it if you fail to repay on time.

The pawnbrokers of medieval Italy worked out an accommodation with the church. To get around the biblical edict against usury, they imposed a "storage charge" on top of a lending charge. Moving on to other lands and cutting deals with dukes and princes, Italian pawnbrokers carved out something close to a monopoly over the pawnshop business of Western Europe. But moneylending remained a controversial activity, and as feudal authority waned, municipal governments decided to enter the business, running pawnshops on a nonprofit basis and keeping charges low to protect the poor from being exploited. This tradition continues in a few places, including Mexico City, down to the present day.[1]

In the United States, pawnshops were commercial enterprises

from the start. But they had an egalitarian dimension. Until the nineteenth century, they were the banks for communities that did not have banks and often the only source of consumer credit available to African Americans and other minorities.[2] Even now, there are pawnbrokers who speak with pride of offering a needed service at a fair price—with pride and with some truth, when you compare them to a few of the other business forms that make up the universe of "alternative financial services."

"U R APPROVED—WE LOVE BAD CREDIT"

That's what the sign said over the lot in Batavia, New York, where twenty-two-year-old Michael Alvarez—soon to start a job at a Ponderosa steakhouse—decided to go car shopping. He didn't consult his mother because he knew what she would say: "Wait. Buy a car when you can afford one."

Alicia Alvarez has strong feelings about financial responsibility—and about loans. As the manager of a community credit union in Rochester, she has heard horror stories about so-called buy here, pay here car dealers like the one where her son, without her knowledge, bought his green 1998 Saturn.

Michael's experience did nothing to improve her opinion of these places. One of the Saturn's outside mirrors had fallen off before he left the lot. The tailpipe was wrapped in aluminum foil to hide the rust. The car didn't seem to like going into reverse, and, once in, it would sometimes pop right back out. Those were comparatively minor issues, though, compared to the fact that Michael had set out to buy an entirely different car—a red 2000 Chevrolet Cavalier. He had already signed the loan papers, he told his mother, when the salesman explained that, based on a closer review of his finances, he "couldn't afford" the Cavalier.

The car wasn't the only thing that had been switched on him. Going over the paperwork with his mother, Michael realized that what he had thought was a loan from a local bank actually came from a finance company on Long Island, and the interest rate was 24.75 percent, not the 10 percent he had been led to expect.

A week later, he returned to the lot with both his parents, to see if he could cancel the purchase. Impossible, the manager said. He would fix the transmission and the mirror, but the loan was out of his control. Or so he firmly insisted until Alicia Alvarez mentioned what she does for a living and brought some of her knowledge of the law to bear on the situation. Taking out Michael's copy of the loan agreement, she pointed to a clause stating that the finance company still had "recourse." That, as she and the lot manager both knew, meant that if Michael failed to pay, the finance company would throw the loan right back in the dealer's lap.

They left a short while later with a letter acknowledging the return of the vehicle and promising that Michael would not be sued for nonpayment of the loan. Michael was still out his $500 down payment, which he had borrowed from his girlfriend's mother. But he and his parents felt that he had made a lucky escape, even so.[3]

Buy here, pay here car lots, auto title lenders, payday lenders, refund-anticipation lenders, rent-to-own stores—they all have one thing in common: a vulnerable customer base. Alternative lenders are for people who have no alternatives, or think they don't. Some may be young and impulsive, others merely poor and desperate. Either way, many of those who patronize such businesses are inclined to focus on the here and now, skipping over the provisions of a loan that might have consequences down the road or around the corner. It is a mind-set that can, and regularly does, lead to disaster.

In 2005, James Haga of Marion, Virginia, took out a $1,600 loan from an auto title lender. As he told the story to a reporter for *USA Today,* Haga wound up losing his $13,000 Ford truck on top of $4,500 in payments he had made while he could. Auto title lenders are pawnbrokers for cars, with a twist: while the lender lays legal claim to ownership of the property, the property itself remains with the borrower. It is a huge business, especially in the South and the Southwest, and many people do lose their cars— seventeen thousand Tennesseans in the year 2004 alone.[4]

But auto title loans can be ruinously expensive whether or not the vehicle is seized. In Valdosta, Georgia, Gwen Irvin put up her 1995 Cadillac as collateral on an $1,800 loan. To come up with an eventual $6,000 in payments, she sold her TV, her VCR, and other valued possessions one after another. "We were stuck in a situation that was really endless, every month scrounging around . . . ," she explained, "so we wouldn't have to walk."[5]

MAKING THE UNAFFORDABLE SEEM AFFORDABLE

Howard Karger, who teaches social policy at the University of Houston, writes about a variety of alternative lending institutions in his book *Shortchanged: Life and Debt in the Fringe Economy.* In their different ways, he concludes, they are all in the business of "making the unaffordable seem affordable."[6]

One method is to blur the line between credit costs and other costs. The interest rate on Michael Alvarez's car loan was 24.75 percent—already sky-high by automobile-financing standards. The price of his Saturn, with taxes and fees and a six-month, 6,000-mile warranty, was listed as $5,007, which required him to take out a $4,507 loan on top of his $500 down payment. At $240 per month for twenty-four months, he would be paying over $6,000 for a car with a Blue Book value of about $1,700.[7]

The price of a car, in other words, becomes a very elastic thing in situations like these. Buy here, pay here dealers normally do not post prices on their vehicles; sometimes they don't even have a price in mind until they have sized up the prospective customer. One large national chain, JD Byrider, relies on a computer program that it calls Automated Risk Evaluator (ARE) to calculate the maximum that someone can afford; only then does the company set a price.[8]

The line between the cost of a product and the cost of credit can be just as fuzzy in the rent-to-own business. These companies generally specialize in furniture and appliances. Let's say your TV stops working and you can't afford a replacement. A rent-to-own store might give you a television worth $200 for seventy-eight weekly payments of $9.99. Technically, it's a lease with an option to buy. That distinction is legally important, allowing rent-to-own stores to get around the interest caps and other consumer finance rules of many states; the idea of renting may appeal to some customers as well. "Ten dollars a week," you say to yourself. "Not bad." But by the time you've made all those payments (assuming you don't incur any late-payment penalties, which would be unusual), that $200 TV will cost you $779.[9] That's hundreds of dollars more than you would pay using a credit card—even the highest-interest credit card currently in existence.

Refund-anticipation loans are another case where the cost of credit becomes difficult to disentangle from other costs. These loans are generally brokered by tax preparers, who charge separately for their accounting work. Usually they receive a fee for setting up the loan; some collect another fee for cashing the refund check. For these combined services, a client might end up paying as much as $800 or $900 on a $2,100 refund.[10]

Refund-anticipation loans grew exponentially during the 1990s, with the expansion of the earned income tax credit (EITC).[11] The EITC is supposed to boost the incomes of low-wage workers. It's an antipoverty program—the only one, says Jean Ann Fox of the Consumer Federation of America, "where the cost of distribution is imposed on the recipients."[12] Refund-anticipation loans are extremely expensive if measured in terms of annualized interest. With the IRS now delivering most refunds within a week or two, however, the absolute cost is small, and easily overlooked alongside the other charges on a tax preparer's bill. Because some companies promote the service as an "instant refund," some customers only half-realize that they are taking out a loan in the first place.[13]

ENDLESS EMERGENCY

Alternative lending is what's known as a countercyclical industry—one that does well when the general economy does poorly, and vice versa. The conditions of the past several decades—rising inequality, increased economic insecurity for middle- as well as lower-income families—have been good for business. In the post-war era, pawnbroking, for example, looked like it might be a dying industry. But after a long and steady decline, the number of pawnshops in the United States has tripled since 1985, going from about 5,000 to an estimated 14,000.[14]

This resurgence has come about partly through stepped-up marketing to the traditional alternative-lending customer base—the poor. It also reflects an intensified effort to appeal to middle-income Americans. It may be symptomatic of our times that payday lending, the fastest-growing form of alternative lending (at least until very recently), requires its customers to have regular paychecks and bank accounts.

The typical payday loan is for a few hundred dollars and fourteen to eighteen days. (The due date may be the borrower's actual payday or a few days later.)[15] Payday lending started out as a sideline of the check-cashing business. Today, it's a booming industry in its own right, taking in an estimated $6 billion in annual revenues.[16] While the country has more pawnshops than McDonald's outlets, the number of payday loan stores (twenty-five thousand according to one recent estimate) exceeds all the McDonald's, Burger King, and Wendy's combined.[17]

To get a loan, you submit a couple of pay stubs or other evidence of employment, along with a postdated personal check or electronic withdrawal authorization for the combined principal and interest. Interest rates are usually in the neighborhood of 15 percent—15 percent for two weeks. To get a $300 loan, in other words, you would write a check for $345.

The check serves mainly as a repayment motivator. The borrower is expected to return to the store by the due date and settle the loan either in cash or through a direct debit agreement; otherwise, the payday lender deposits the original check. If that happens, the borrower faces a bounced-check charge on top of the loan charge.[18]

Critics of payday lending, who are numerous, point out that a 15 percent charge for a two-week loan works out to the equivalent of a 390 percent annual interest rate, which is getting into loan-shark territory.[19] (In fact, it puts some loan sharks to shame. The suspects in one recent Justice Department loan-sharking investigation were charging 1 to 5 percent a week; even at the high end, that works out to a mere 270 percent in annual terms.)[20]

Such comparisons are grossly unfair, industry leaders say. "To reach the triple digit APRs quoted by our critics, a consumer would have to renew an advance over and over," one big payday loan company protests on the "Myths vs. Reality" page of its Web site.[21] Unfortunately, many customers do just that. In 2005, while working as a cashier on Hilton Head Island, South Carolina, Lakisissha Thomas took out a $400 payday loan. By the end of 2006, she had paid over $2,500 for her original $400. (While her debt accumulated, Thomas told a reporter for BusinessWeek, she never really thought much about "what do you call it—interest?")[22]

Some payday lenders will close out one loan before issuing another. For borrowers, these back-to-back transactions can be confusing: "Though they have to repay the first loan before taking out the second loan, the second loan can seem like 'new money' since they walk out with cash in their pocket like the first time," the Center for Responsible Lending observed in a 2006 report. "In reality, they are borrowing back their own money minus the fee, still paying $50 every payday to keep defaulting on their $300 loan."[23]

Lisa Engelkins, a single mother earning less than $8 an hour, wound up renewing thirty-five times. Over a span of seventeen months, Engelkins paid $1,254 in fees on a $255 loan. "I had no idea how this trap worked until I was out from under it," she said later.[24]

By characterizing their product as an "emergency loan," payday lenders have won exemption from the interest limits that many states impose on other consumer loans. But, as study after study has shown, the one-time loan is an almost mythical exception to the rule. Very few payday loans get renewed twenty-six straight times (many states limit the number of renewals, in any case). Close to 90 percent of all borrowers renew at least once a year, however.[25] In Illinois, the average (according to a study conducted by the Illinois Department of Financial Institutions) was thirteen times. Sometimes a customer will patronize more than one payday lender in order to get around the rules.[26]

Like late fees for the credit card industry, renewals (or rollovers or back-to-back loans) are what sustain the payday loan business. That's the conclusion not only of industry critics but of sympathetic observers like the financial analysts at Ernst & Young who, after examining data from nineteen Canadian payday lending firms, wrote that "the survival of payday loan operators depends on establishing and maintaining a substantial repeat customer base."[27] The Federal Deposit Insurance Corporation's Center for Financial Research looked at the industry in the United States and put it more bluntly: "We find that high-frequency borrowers account for a disproportionate share of a payday loan store's loans and profits."[28]

AN AGE OF GIANTS

Alternative lending used to be a mom-and-pop business. Today it is fast becoming a world of corporate chains. In the pawnshop field, Jack Daugherty started out in the early 1970s with a single shop in Irving, Texas. Daugherty went on to found Cash America, which, after swallowing up rivals with names like SuperPawn and Cashland, now operates some 450 pawnshops in twenty-one states. In 2006, Cash America's profits came to $690 million.[29] Another big chain, EZ Pawn, has 280 shops in eleven states.[30]

Cash America and EZ Pawn have counterparts in other alternative-lending subspecialties. In the rent-to-own field, Rent-A-Center leads the way, with 3,500 stores in all fifty states plus the District of Columbia and Puerto Rico. Aaron Rents comes in second, with 1,380 stores. In auto title lending, LoanMax makes half a million loans a year through 200-odd stores in twenty-one states. In the buy here, pay here car business, JD Byrider has 130 lots in thirty states (with plans to open hundreds more).[31]

Concentration is an old story when it comes to refund-anticipation loans. These loans, dispensed in many cases by H&R Block, Jackson Hewitt, and other tax preparers, ultimately come from a handful of banks; in 2000, one bank alone—Household—accounted for an estimated 80 percent of the business.[32]

In check cashing and payday lending, the consolidation story is also a product diversification story. Two of the giants, ACE Cash Express and Dollar Financial, are in the payday loan business where the law allows; elsewhere, they focus on check cashing and a smorgasbord of other sevices, such as money orders, utility payments, and the sale of phone cards and lottery tickets. In 2004,

ACE had more than 1,200 stores.[33] Dollar Financial's stores, which operate under the names Money Mart, Loan Mart, and Money Shop, also do electronic tax filing and prepaid Visa debit cards. Together, ACE and Dollar Financial control about one-fifth of the country's check-cashing outlets.[34]

The chains command financial resources far beyond those of the independent, locally based lenders they are displacing. Many of these companies have ongoing relationships with major banks. Byrider, for example, has a $110 million revolving credit line from Bank of America, while the Royal Bank of Canada provides financing for Aaron Rents.[35] Behind the giants of the converging payday lending and check-cashing world stand JPMorgan Chase, Wells Fargo, Wachovia, and Bank of America.[36] In addition, Wells Fargo and U.S. Bancorp have entered the payday loan field themselves.

The payday lending industry has received crucial strategic and legal as well as financial help from the banking industry. In the early 1980s and 1990s, payday lenders got a huge boost from a series of deals in which they, in effect, "rented" banks' court-approved immunity from state usury laws. Over a vital span of years in which payday lending grew into the huge industry it is today, this legal ploy was a key element of the business plan.[37]

Most of these companies are publicly traded, giving them access to the financial markets, where alternative lending has, in recent years, been seen as a field of high promise. In other words, the corporatization of alternative lending has produced a national industry with deep pockets and the ability to engage in a kind of marketing that the alternative-lending world had not seen before. They're using those resources to sell their products—check cashing, payday loans, auto title loans—and something more.

FACE-LIFT

In early 2007, a very strange series of advertisements began airing on American television. A bus driver starred in one spot, a gym teacher in another, a waiter in a third. The theme of all these ads was that Americans with jobs like these sometimes need a little help paying their bills. And they deserve help, because, as all the ads ended by saying to these underappreciated, overworked, and undercompensated mainstays of the economy: "You advance America."

The ads don't say a lot about the company or its product line. The underlying message seems to be: "Maybe you've heard some unflattering things about businesses like ours. Maybe you've heard stories about people being misled, overcharged, and exploited; and yes, maybe there were companies that acted that way. But not us. We're different. We're just another all-American industry. We're on *your* side."

Why does this need to be said? The answer may go back to a remarkable report on the payday lending industry and its impact on Americans employed in another underpaid field of endeavor: soldiering. Issued in 2006 by the U.S. Department of Defense, the report concluded that payday loans had become a problem so grave as to "undermine military readiness."[38] That finding led Congress, on September 30, 2006, to pass a law setting a 36 percent annual interest rate cap on all loans issued by companies operating near American military facilities. The legislation brought a sudden end to payday lending at Seymour Johnson Air Force Base and Fort Bragg in North Carolina, Point Loma Naval Base in San Diego, and many other military base communities where payday lenders

had proliferated.[39] For the industry, though, the immediate financial impact, large as it was, paled beside the momentum the law
gave to opponents of payday lending across the country.

Twelve states, as well as Puerto Rico and the Virgin Islands,
have banned payday lending outright. Others have passed significant restrictions. By early 2007, bans or limits were on the legislative docket in a number of the states where payday lending
remained lawful. If payday lending undermined military readiness, many people seemed to be thinking, maybe the time had
come to rethink its effects on the nonuniformed population.

This is an industry, in short, with a serious public relations
problem. It has responded with a determined effort to present a
new face to the world, and no company has worked harder at that
task than the Spartanburg, South Carolina–based giant, Advance
America.

Advance America was cofounded by George Johnson and
William M. Webster. Both came out of the franchise world: Johnson had made his fortune in video rental; Webster in fried
chicken. Both had been active in politics: Johnson served three
terms in the South Carolina state legislature; Webster worked at
the Education Department and the White House during the Clinton years. Casting an aura of wholesome legitimacy was part of
the business plan from the outset. The company, according to its
Web site, is committed to "providing full disclosure to customers,
complying with all state and federal laws, advertising truthfully,
encouraging and promoting consumer responsibility and championing other specifications to help regulate the industry."[40] Advance America and its cofounders have played a conspicuous part
in programs to help the disadvantaged—collecting school sup-

plies for needy students; funding minority scholarships; conducting financial literacy programs; registering voters; mentoring women and minority business owners; and supporting the Girl Scouts, the NAACP, and the Urban League.[41]

To judge by some of the company's press materials, you'd think it was a charity that did a little lending on the side. Nevertheless, in less than a decade, Advance America has become a huge company, with 2,800 locations in thirty-six states. When it became a publicly traded corporation in 2005, cofounder Webster made $20 million by selling just 15 percent of his stock holdings.[42]

That huge haul rested on a perception of payday lending as a high-growth, sky's-the-limit kind of business. Now, a cloud of doubt has descended. Financial analysts, fund managers, and other Wall Street heavyweights have begun to wonder: Which way is this industry going? Up fast? Or down fast?

Up, say those dewy TV spots. Forget what the Department of Defense said. Disregard the measures recently enacted in Arkansas, Connecticut, Georgia, Maine, Maryland, Massachusetts, New Jersey, New York, North Carolina, Pennsylvania, Vermont, West Virginia, Puerto Rico, and the Virgin Islands. Sure, some people haven't kept up with the times. They still associate us with those dusty, grimy, exploitative lending institutions of yesteryear. They haven't gotten the message yet—but they will.

To help make that forecast come true, alternative lenders have been spending heavily on lobbying and campaign contributions, especially in states like Arkansas, where the industry's fate has been looking shaky. In February 2007, an industry group launched a $10 million public education campaign, featuring TV ads entreating people to "please borrow only what you feel comfortable paying back when it's due." ("Some of our customers didn't understand the intent of our product—it's not a long-term financial solution," one industry leader explained.) No fewer than 164 leading payday lenders and other alternative lenders (including Cash America, Check Into Cash, Dollar Financial Group, Express Check Advance, First Cash Financial Services, and Rent-A-Center) committed themselves to offering an extended repayment plan with an eight-week no-fee grace period, and, as another element of their "customer pledge," said they would include warning notices in "all marketing and advertising materials" clearly stating that payday loans "are for short-term use only." They promised to refrain in the future from advertising such loans "for frivolous uses."[43]

It was all part of an effort, as one industry leader put it, to "address the small number of customers who misuse the product or become overreliant on it, and put themselves in financial jeopardy."[44] Yet, while these new practices were being promoted with a $10 million marketing campaign, including commercials on BET, the Food Network, and other channels, other developments had a business-as-usual flavor. In Arkansas, payday lenders were trying to evade a new payday-lending law through more of the old rent-a-bank agreements that federal regulators had seemingly rejected. In Pennsylvania, Advance America responded to the state's ban on payday loans by devising a new credit line that, as Governor Ed Rendell said (while his attorney general filed a suit to block the plan), was an "outrageous product" in which someone borrowing $500 and making minimum payments of $20 a month would end up paying $4,000 over two years.

Not very long ago, the industry was cruising along on a wave of approval and acclaim from Wall Street and the financial markets. Now it's worried and struggling to regain its momentum. The question remains: Will payday lenders and other such businesses be willing to turn their backs on the tradition of aggressive marketing, confusing terms, and other blandishments that, as recently as 2005, created an average of eight loans per year per customer for two of the leaders, Advance America and QC Holdings, adding up to a return of $793 on a $325 loan?[45] The answer, based on the evidence to date, is: We may be willing to go far, but not quite that far.

UNITED AND SEPARATE

Alternative and mainstream lending used to be separate worlds. Now they are bound together by a web of partnerships, credit lines, investment links, and other ties. This could ultimately be a positive development, in the view of some consumer advocates, if it leads to financial institutions offering a broad range of services for a broad range of customers—cashing checks and extending low-cost credit to low-income people while, at the same time, giving them access to savings accounts and helping them move up the ladder to the kind of lower-cost credit and other financial services enjoyed by middle- and upper-income Americans. So far, though, there has been little sign of that. Despite all the convergence on the back end, customers still face two very different front ends. Upwards of 50 million Americans "have no relationship to mainstream financial service providers," according to a study by the Fannie Mae Foundation and the Urban Institute.[46] The problem of the "unbanked" is partly one of accessability; many people live and work in communities like west Baltimore, which have been all but abandoned by the banking industry, and where check-cashing shops, payday lenders, and other alternative lending institutions abound. In Los Angeles, 61 percent of all households live within one mile of a payday lender, with the percentage varying from 42 percent for white non-Hispanics to 76 percent for African Americans and 70 percent for Hispanics.[47]

Across the country, African American neighborhoods have three times more payday lending stores per capita than do comparable white communities (controlled for income, home ownership, poverty, unemployment rate, location, age, education, and gender).[48] In California, according to a study conducted by the California Reinvestment Coalition, wealthy cities have an average of three check-cashing outlets and fifty-five bank branches, while lower-income cities have seven banks and twenty-four check-cashing outlets.[49]

But the problem goes beyond geography. In fact, many alternative-lending customers live and work in neighborhoods with banks, and many have bank accounts. Even among those who do, however, many have developed a well-justified feeling that banks are not meeting their needs in any affordable way.

In an earlier era, banks welcomed small depositors, including teenagers who, with their families' encouragement, came in with $10, $20, or $30 to put into a savings account as a first step along a lifetime path of financial responsibility. Nowadays, minimum-deposit requirements and service charges make bank accounts inhospitable not just to teenagers but to many adults who cannot afford to leave thousands of dollars in their accounts on a steady basis. Thus, even as many banks have become partners or supporters of alternative lenders, they are helping create the conditions that lead people, by default, to patronize these institutions.

In defense of their practices, payday lenders insist that they give many customers a better deal than do banks, with their minimum deposits and service charges and bounced-check fees. "If it only cost $10 to bounce a check, I'm not sure we would have nearly as big a payday loan industry," says Dollar Financial's Donald Gerhardt.[50] And he's right.

But it does not necessarily follow that payday lenders "enhance the economic well-being of people," as Garhardt goes on to say. A more accurate conclusion might be that banks and payday lenders alike are systematically taking advantage of low-income customers.

Despite the growing financial intimacy of banks and alternative lenders, some industry observers see evidence of increased stratification in the financial services world. Borrowing costs more for those who have little money to begin with—that is true in both absolute and relative terms—and recent studies suggest a widening gap between what the poor pay and what others pay. Based on Federal Reserve data, *Business Week* estimates that in 1989 the interest rate on auto loans for households earning up to $30,000 a year was 16.8 percent higher than for households earning over $90,000 a year. By 2004, the difference was 56.1 percent. The data indicate a similar pattern in other areas of lending. "It's not only that the poor are paying more," says FDIC chair Sheila Bair. "The poor are paying a lot more."[51]

The financial services industry has built a system of "banks for the middle class and check cashers for the poor," as lawyer Anne

Kim wrote in a report for the Chicago Federal Reserve Bank a few years ago. "Access to savings tools for the middle class but barriers to savings for the poor. Low-cost financial services for the middle class and high fee-based services for the poor."[52] Low-income people pay more for loans whether they get them from auto title lenders, payday lenders, or banks. The new, consolidated financial services industry seems to be a lot like the old mom-and-pop industry in its commitment to keeping tens of millions of Americans locked in a world off high-cost, hard-to-escape credit.

9

THE END OF THE ROPE

Repo men pounding on your door at five in the morning. Collection agents robo-calling you at home and work. Sham credit counselors who promise to help but find a way to make a bad situation even worse. These are just a few of the wretched experiences that define the lives of Americans in the final throes of unmanageable debt. Lenders may have lost interest in you as a viable customer for further credit, but take heart! You have just begun to have value in the eyes of a whole slew of other professionals—debt collectors, debt counselors, and bankruptcy court judges. By the time they're finished with you, you may find yourself wishing that debtor's prison had never been abolished. It would be a lot more peaceful.

SEXY BUSINESS

In 2006, according to Experian, one of the three big credit reporting agencies, 20 million Americans were three months or more past due on their credit card bills, while 40 million were past due on other kinds of credit accounts such as home, car, student loans, and bills for medical services or utilities.[1] It is numbers like these that, according to one industry leader, make debt collection one of the "sexiest" and "most financially lucrative businesses you can get into."[2]

It is a business that has been through a profound transformation over the past ten years. The old-school model of debt collection largely consisted of in-house operations and third-party debt collectors. Third-party debt collectors are private agencies or law firms that service accounts on behalf of credit card companies, health care providers, and a wide array of other clients. These people make money only if they are successful in collecting money from the debtor, taking as their fee a percentage of the amount collected.

They're supposed to be regulated by the Federal Trade Commission and are obligated to follow rules outlined in the Fair Debt Collection Practices Act (FDCPA). But with small enforcement budgets, the FTC has been essentially powerless in its ability to protect consumers. This has become especially true as the number of debt collection agencies has risen to 6,500 in 2007.[3] Fueling the growth of the debt-collecting industry are debt buyers; debt purchasing is a relatively new practice whose roots trace back to the early 1990s, when the federal government began selling off assets from failed savings and loans.[4] Today, there are more than five hundred debt-buying firms, up from about a dozen in 1996.[5]

Here's how it works. Today, credit card companies will sell their bad debts—debts they have already written off the books—to debt buyers for just pennies on the dollar. The debt buyers then break up the debt into smaller chunks and resell them to collection agencies, who then try to collect the old debts for more pennies on the dollar than they paid. The growing profitability of just one of the publicly traded debt-buying firms illustrates how buying and then collecting debt for pennies on the dollar has become a million-dollar profit-making enterprise.

According to the *Boston Globe*, Portfolio Recovery Associates, based in Norfolk, Virginia, purchased 658 debt portfolios with a face value of $16.4 billion over the last decade—paying just $415.4 million, or about 2.5 cents for each dollar of bad debt it purchased. In turn, it collected on average 7.5 cents per dollar from this old debt. At first, profits were relatively small. The company made $402,000 in 1998. But the debt-buying business has exploded as more creditors sell off their bad debt, and Portfolio Recovery turned a profit of $36.8 million in 2005.[6]

As debt collecting has became more profitable, the tactics have become both more aggressive and inscrutable. In 2005, consumers filed 66,257 complaints against debt collectors, up from 13,950 in 2000.[7] In fact, the FTC receives more complaints about debt collectors than about any other industry. The bulk of the complaints—42.7 percent—charged that debt collectors were misrepresenting the amount, nature, or legal status of a debt by demanding a larger payment than was permitted by law—a violation of the FDCPA. The second most common set of complaints was about harassment. In 2005, 14,352 consumers said that collectors had harassed them by calling repeatedly or continuously. Another 8,000 consumers complained about collectors who had used obscene or profane language.

Debt collectors have been known to call neighbors, employers, and anyone else who may be able to help them track down their prey. Stories abound about calls made to people at work and to family members and friends. Francis Buselli told the *Washington Post* that he kept receiving calls from a debt collector about a debt they said his daughter owed—his daughter who had moved out of the house over fifteen years ago.[8] On one day, the collectors called six times in fifteen minutes, waiting until the last call to put the final screws in. That's when they recited his Social Security number, mentioned his wife by name, and (Buselli said) threatened to send someone over to beat him up.

Then there are the repeated calls seeking payments on debts that were never owed. Mary H. Monroe, a seventy-one-year-old retiree in Williamsburg, Brooklyn, received a succession of calls about an $8,000 debt from tuition and fees at a beauty school she had never attended.[9] Mistakes are made all the time in the business, and it's the consumers who pay the price in extra fines, fees, and, most dramatically, with the seizure of their property. Many people wake up to an early-morning beating on the door, with a tow truck waiting to seize their car. Often, they have not received a letter informing them that the debt was under collection or that they were being sued for failing to repay.

How does this happen? Those letters may have gone to the wrong address, maybe an address that is years out of date. This was the experience of Marie-Colette Dimanche, as she told the *Boston Globe*. At six o'clock one morning, a man and a woman showed up at her door demanding either $2,000 for an old credit card debt or her keys. They had court documents authorizing them to seize her car. But Dimanche eventually discovered that the debt collector had supplied the court with an address where she hadn't lived for more than a decade.

The *Globe* series turned up numerous stories like this. The problem is, debt collectors aren't obligated to show the courts that they have the right address. To get a seizure order, they simply submit *an* address and proof that the letters were sent with no response from the debtor. When it comes time to execute an order, though, the industry seems to have a better record of finding out where people really live. The obligation to right the wrong falls on consumers, who must take legal action to retrieve their property and pay the expense.

Debt collection lawsuits have been on the rise. Between 2000 and 2005, there was one debt collection lawsuit for every five Massachusetts households. In 2004 alone, debt collectors filed twenty thousand lawsuits in Allen County, Indiana—one for every six households.[10]

Wall Street is very enamored of the debt collection industry these days. According to *Business Week,* in the third quarter of 2005 alone, private equity firms, venture capitalists, and others invested $1.6 billion in the business. In September 2005, Citigroup's venture capital funds bought a controlling stake in Receivable Management Services Corp., a Pennsylvania firm that specializes in business debts. The student lender Sallie Mae bought a company that buys bad mortgage debt.[11] Big backing by Wall Street ensures that this $15 billion a year industry will continue to grow.

And if you are saddled with tax debt, don't expect a call from the IRS. In 2004, the federal government authorized the IRS to "outsource" its tax debt collection to private firms. With an estimated $270 billion in outstanding tax payments, aggressive collection tactics are likely, given that the debt collectors stand to make 25 percent of any collection in revenues.[12]

Although the federal government has assured taxpayers that

their rights will be protected, the FTC has already proven it does not have the resources to adequately protect consumers. Bringing in the private debt collection industry, with an already nefarious reputation, to do the government's bidding ensures that debt collectors will continue to harass, abuse, and ruin the lives of many individuals and their families.

SAVE US FROM OUR PROTECTORS

Before the debt collectors come after you—while you still have some hope of avoiding bankruptcy—you may be tempted to seek help from one of the thousands of credit counseling agencies in business today. Credit counselors have been around for a long time. In the past, however, it was generally fairly easy to distinguish between the people who made their living by getting you into debt and those who made their living getting you out of debt. Now, increasingly often, they all seem to use similar practices. In a few cases, they even turn out to be arms of the same corporate entities. The key point, in any case, is that here, too, the borrower must beware; reputable, nonprofit counseling agencies still exist, but scam-filled, profit-seeking hucksters abound.

A ride on any mass transit vehicle confirms that helping people "repair their credit" and "get out of debt quick" has become a huge business for corporate America and a risky business for consumers. This wasn't always the case.

The original credit counseling agencies have their roots in the 1960s. They were established by lenders and credit card companies looking to combat a rise in personal bankruptcies. The vast majority of agencies were screened and approved by one national organization, the National Foundation for Credit Counseling (NFCC), and were community-based, nonprofit organizations. NFCC members offered a very straightforward personalized service. They employed trained counselors. These counselors sat down one-on-one with consumers, guided them through budgeting, and helped them develop the financial strategy that best met their needs.

Many consumers opted for what's called a debt management plan. Under such a plan, a consumer consolidated all of his or her unsecured debt under one credit counseling agency. The consumer then became responsible for making a single payment to that agency and trusted the organization to distribute the appropriate monthly payments to each of his or her creditors on time. Credit counselors negotiated with each of a consumer's creditors and ensured that late fees were waived and interest rates were lowered.

This was how debt management worked until just a few years ago. Creditors recovered payments they would likely have lost otherwise. Consumers found much-needed relief. Credit counseling agencies could be trusted. They were part of local communities and had a strong nonprofit mission. They met their operating expenses by charging creditors 12 to 15 percent of the funds they regained or by requesting small contributions from their consumers.[13]

Credit counseling began to lose its nonprofit way in the late 1990s. That was when the rules of the game changed. Consumer debt ballooned, creating a large market for credit counseling agencies, and unscrupulous vendors, who were nonprofit on paper but greedy in practice, blossomed. In the early 1990s, there were about two hundred credit counseling agencies in the United States. Ninety percent of them were affiliated with the NFCC and were true to its high standards and mission. Today there are more than one thousand agencies, and only about 10 percent are NFCC members.

As the number of credit counseling agencies increased dramatically and lost their NFCC connection, they lost their community-based focus. In a few short years, the debt management plan has gone from being a viable option for consumers to a dangerous trap.

Fast forward to today. The "nonprofit" credit counseling industry is now a $1 billion-a-year business—one that is coming under increasing scrutiny from watchdog groups, the IRS, and Congress. It is about time. Estimates show that nearly 9 million Americans have some contact with a consumer credit counseling agency each year.[14] Many are left poorer—quite literally—for the experience.

Today dubious nonprofit credit counseling agencies use the Internet, direct mail, and telemarketing to hook consumers. Face-to-face advice tailored to improve financial well-being has been replaced by fast talk and cookie-cutter debt consolidation solutions.

On a consumer affairs Web site, "Wayne" of Gainesville, Florida, described his experience with DebtFree America, a credit counseling firm that, by his account, delivered little service and charged exorbitantly for it. Wayne and his wife had a long history of good credit. When they fell on hard times, they decided to work with DebtFree America to get things back under control.

They paid a $539 fee up front, and trusted DebtFree America to make monthly payments on their behalf. After a few months, the couple discovered they had been ripped off. DebtFree America not only failed to help them lower their interest rates, "They actually ruined our credit by not sending the correct amount of money for the payments and being late, which in turn cost us $70 in late fees. We canceled the service, but they refused to reimburse us our $539. We feel as though they didn't live up to their promises and we should receive our money back," says Wayne with disgust.[15]

Unscrupulous debt counseling agencies have defrauded thousands of consumers, earning billons in the process. Maria, another victim, had the misfortune of getting involved with the National Consumer Council, a supposed nonprofit credit counselor in good standing. The National Consumer Council connected Maria to Solidium Credit Recovery Services. Solidium set up a debt management plan that was supposed to help Maria with her debt problems. Instead, the company only made things worse.

After ten months, Maria had paid Solidium nearly $10,000. As part of the deal, she also had to pay London Financial, a Solidium partner, a 3 percent engagement fee, a $1.82 monthly establishment fee, and a $90 monthly service fee. Maria's total outstanding debt when she contacted the National Consumer Council was $106,000. Because of fees directly associated with entering into credit counseling, her total debt soon climbed to $120,000. After nearly a year of credit counseling, Maria was in a daze: "I was told that only one account has been partially settled. I have no idea what I have in my trust account at this date. . . . I do not know if my creditors have been contacted with any offers and I am scared of what can happen next," she reported nervously.[16]

Maria had every right to be nervous. Soon after she told her story to Consumer Affairs, the Federal Trade Commission accused the supposedly nonprofit National Consumer Council and its for-profit affiliates (including the London Financial Group, the National Consumer Debt Council, and Solidium) of "misrepresentations and omissions." A federal judge ordered the National Consumer Council to close its doors forever. The FTC said that National Consumer was "masquerading as a nonprofit debt negotiation organization" and charged that it had "made millions of dollars deceiving consumers into enrolling in their debt negotiation program by promising to reduce their debts," when in fact it did not.[17]

One of the most notorious examples of credit counseling run amok is AmeriDebt. The Maryland-based company was once one of the nation's largest and most widely advertised credit counseling firms.[18] With nearly four hundred thousand customers since 1997, AmeriDebt billed itself as a "nationally recognized nonprofit" and "one of the fastest-growing credit counseling organizations in America."[19] On the surface, AmeriDebt resembled other such firms; it enrolled customers in debt management plans and promised financial education and debt reduction through payment consolidation and reduced interest rates. Its "main goal" was to "help educate Americans on how to reduce, manage, and eliminate their debt." AmeriDebt's practices, however, fell far short of its promises.

Jim Reed of Philadelphia, who told his story to the *Washington Post*, was among nearly two hundred beleaguered AmeriDebt customers who filed complaints against the company in 2001.[20] Reed had made his first payment of $456, believing that AmeriDebt would distribute the funds to his lenders. But when he started incurring late fees and saw his interest rates rise, Reed knew something was up. It turned out that the "voluntary contribution" charged by AmeriDebt wasn't voluntary after all, and customers were rarely, if ever, told that their whole first payment went directly to AmeriDebt. Just four months after signing with AmeriDebt, Reed's debt had ballooned by $5,000.

Widespread dissatisfaction with the industry, and particularly with AmeriDebt, prompted Congress and regulatory agencies to take action. Although AmeriDebt masqueraded as a nonprofit, Senate investigators found that the company—launched by Pamela Shuster in 1997—had been funneling its proceeds to DebtWorks Inc., a for-profit company started by Shuster's husband in 1999.[21] DebtWorks processed accounts from at least eleven other "nonprofit" credit counseling agencies, each of which was affiliated with or "organized by insiders of AmeriDebt." Two months later, the FTC filed a lawsuit against AmeriDebt, alleging that in addition to illegally funneling $2.2 million in profits to for-profit ventures like DebtWorks, AmeriDebt provided no credit counseling services and used hidden fees, which it described as "voluntary," to siphon off nearly $172 million from funds that many customers expected to go to lenders.[22] AmeriDebt has since filed for bankruptcy and agreed to shut down its operations and pay $35 million in restitution.[23]

No matter how many of these scams get exposed and closed down, the list of fraudulent debt-counseling services continues to grow. In 2006 the IRS announced the results of a two-year audit of forty-one tax-exempt credit counseling agencies. As of May 2006, the IRS had terminated or was in the process of terminating the tax-exempt status of all forty-one of them, finding that all were "preying on people who are at their most vulnerable" and engaging in "a herding of people . . . into a debt management plan designed to generate fees."[24]

THE VERY END

Today, more Americans succumb to bankruptcy than to divorce. Over the last decade, the number of families going down this path has more than doubled, from 874,642 in 1995 to just over 2 million in 2005.[25]

The reasons for the surge in bankruptcy filings are not especially obscure. One is the immense expansion of credit extended to families in the 1990s. In 2006, there were more than 691 million credit cards in circulation, and they were used in transactions totaling more than $1.8 trillion.[26] As chronicled in Chapter 3, credit card lending has ballooned, with the average family today carrying an average balance of $5,219. Most economists consider the rise in bankruptcy a predictable by-product of flooding the market with credit and the subsequent rising levels of credit card debt.[27]

The second trend that helps explain this phenomenon is the increased vulnerability of middle-income households. Research by Harvard law professor Elizabeth Warren, a bankruptcy expert, has consistently found that the top three reasons families suffer financial collapse are a major medical event, a job loss, or divorce.[28] Why are families more vulnerable today to these events, than, say, thirty years ago? In their book *The Two-Income Trap*,

Elizabeth Warren and Amelia Warren Tyagi show that the typical middle-class family of today—two parents, two kids—has less disposable income than its counterpart of a generation ago.[29] That's despite the fact that today's typical middle-income household has two earners.

Ignoring the evidence, proponents of bankruptcy reform championed their cause by promoting the myth of the "deadbeat" debtor seeking an easy way out. The traditional model of bankruptcy—founded upon the idea that unexpected household financial distress demands some sort of social safety net allowing debtors to get relief and attain a "fresh start"—seems to have lost its moral resonance. According to the deadbeat theory, bankruptcy no longer carries any stigma and profligate middle- and upper-middle-class Americans have been exploiting a permissive system to walk away from debts they could afford to pay.[30]

It is a grossly inaccurate picture. But, nevertheless, it played an important role in building support for a bogus bankruptcy reform law—the Bankruptcy Abuse Prevention and Consumer Protection Act of 2005 (BAPCPA). The new rules sought to crack down on so-called abuses of the system by placing more obstacles in the path of those filing for bankruptcy. Households that could pay something were now supposed to file for Chapter 13 bankruptcy—which sets up a debt payment plan over five years— as opposed to Chapter 7, which allows for complete erasure of applicable debts.

As a result of the new law, there is a new means test to determine whether a household can afford to repay a portion of its debts. The means test is triggered if the filer's income is above the state median, signaling a potential abuser within the system. In addition to the means test, consumers are required to pay a $50 fee for credit counseling before they can officially file their bankruptcy claim. The new law also makes filing more expensive: $299 for Chapter 7, up from $209, and $274 for Chapter 13, up from $194.[31] Because the new law requires more paperwork and verification by bankruptcy attorneys of their client's financial information, attorney fees have also increased.

One thing is certain: the bill has made it more expensive and onerous to declare bankruptcy. More than a year after its passage, it appears that the myth of the deadbeat debtor was just that. It was created and promoted by the credit card companies and allied interests to justify reforming the system. The credit card industry actually drafted the initial legislation in 1997.[32] For eight years, from 1997 until its final passage, the credit card industry spent over $40 million in political fundraising efforts and millions more in lobbying for the reforms—even though the proposal enjoyed broad bipartisan support in both the House and Senate.[33]

In the 1990s, Congress twice sent the bill to President Bill Clinton, who vetoed the legislation both times. It wasn't until 2002, when Republicans controlled both the White House and the Congress, that passage became assured. In the final year of debate, amendments were offered to the legislation that would have strengthened consumer protections against unfair and capricious industry practices, such as banning universal default. All the pro-consumer amendments were jettisoned by Republican-controlled committees.

The bill's supporters hammered away at the theme of personal responsibility, while the practices of the credit card industry went largely unexamined. In this debate, accountability was completely one-sided. Representative Dick Boucher (D-VA) summed up the pro-reform position: "Bankruptcy is becoming a first stop for some, rather than a last resort, as debtors treat bankruptcy as merely another financial planning tool and file for bankruptcy for simple convenience. These practices are permitted under the current bankruptcy law which allows debtors to walk away from their debts regardless of whether they have the ability to pay any portion of what they owe. The legislation which was approved by the House Judiciary Committee today restores personal responsibility to the bankruptcy system by creating a fair, needs-based system for bankruptcy filings."[34]

Republican senator Orrin Hatch from Utah, who had championed the bill for eight years, said at its signing into law, "We are a compassionate nation but we should not be fools. We want to give our neighbors who get in over their heads a chance to get out of their financial troubles. But for some it is a way to avoid personal responsibility. There is something inherently unfair about denying full restitution to creditors."[35]

As predicted, the push for "reform" set off a stampede of bankruptcy filings in the months leading up to the bill's passage in October 2005. Filings of Chapter 7 spiked to over one million in the months before the law took effect, while Chapter 13 filings declined.[36] After a big decrease in both types of filings once the law took force, filings are now starting to rise back to their normal levels.[37] A study by the National Association of Bankruptcy Attorneys finds that the new law doesn't punish deadbeats as it purported to, but rather penalizes those in dire financial straits with higher fees and filing costs. The organization's study found that out of 61,355 consumers who had planned to file for bankruptcy and had completed their mandatory credit counseling visit, 97 percent were deemed unable to repay any debts.[38] In addition, four out of five of these soon-to-be filers were facing financial collapse due to circumstances beyond their control, such as the loss of a job, catastrophic medical expenses, or the death of a spouse.

Phil and Judy Specht of Albuquerque, New Mexico, whose story appeared in *The Nation*, experienced the disastrous consequences of bankruptcy reform firsthand.[39] Phil was a maintenance worker at a retirement community and Judy worked at a local semiconductor plant. For a while, the couple—in their late fifties—made enough to cover their mortgage payments with a little left at the end of the month. But they fell on hard times when Phil was diagnosed with a bone marrow disease and forced to retire early and Judy lost her job and her health coverage. To make matters worse, Judy developed a range of health problems that added to their already spiraling medical expenses.

To save money, the couple began cutting corners. They sold furniture and jewelry, and rationed their pills. Judy stopped taking her cholesterol medication altogether. "I was left with a choice—my medication or a roof over our heads," Judy explained. It turned out that she got neither. With $4,000 in medical bills and $90,000 left to pay on their mortgage, the couple filed for Chapter 7 bankruptcy and eventually lost their home. Even after going bankrupt, the couple had $1,000 in medical bills.

Too often, when households search for financial advice, counseling, or help managing their debts, there awaits not a fresh start or a helping hand, but an aggressive, law-flouting industry of debt collectors and scam-filled "counselors" offering quick and easy schemes that prey on the desperate. At the end of the debt rope, there is no slack. Just a tightening of the knot.

10

ADDRESSING THE DEBT CRISIS

CREDIT CARDS that start out promising zero interest and end up charging 30 percent or more. Student loan debt that lingers into our retirement years. Toxic mortgages that drive families (and neighborhoods) to ruin. Americans are leveraged to the hilt and, in many cases, beyond, with such key indicators as the financial obligations ratio (the portion of monthly income consumed by debt payments) and the debt service ratio (the relationship of debt to personal income) at record highs.[1]

Yet each person's experience feels intensely personal, and many Americans persist in thinking about debt in the language of the self-help authors and the pseudo–credit counselors: as a condition we have brought on ourselves. It's something most people can barely talk about, much less agitate or organize (or vote) about.

Of course, there are things that people can do—and must do—individually. Whether you're sliding into trouble or already deep in it, you'll need to take action, and you may need trustworthy advice first. (A good place to get it is Americans for Fairness in Lending—a coalition of consumer groups that will steer you toward a reputable credit counselor or consumer lawyer wherever you live.)[2]

Debt induces paralysis, which can turn a bad situation into an impossible one. But just as individual profligacy does not explain the problem, individual belt-tightening cannot be a sufficient solution. Over the past several decades, seismic shifts in the economic landscape, along with a fractured public safety net, have made debt the only mechanism available to many Americans for coping with a job loss or a medical emergency or even everyday needs like car repairs and groceries. We borrow as much as we do because, at one key stage of life after another (raising small children, going to college, getting sick and needing medical care, buying a home, retiring), we have been left short. Even that unavoidable "good debt" can turn bad when a college education doesn't lead to a well-paying job or our homes become our only cushion. American homeowners cashed out over $700 billion in equity between 2001 and 2005 to cover living expenses and pay down credit card debt, leaving them owning a smaller portion of their homes and blurring the line between good debt and bad.

The very same ideology that has put us in this economic predicament is behind the policies that give private lenders license to peddle expensive, tricky, hard-to-escape loans. Freed from meaningful regulation, the lending industry stands poised to capitalize on shaky family finances. And capitalize they have.

In an era of economic change, technology has not only radically altered the way we work and live. It has also revolutionized the financial services industry, enabling the development of calibrated categories of risk and tiers of loan charges, ostensibly based on a consumer's credit score and likelihood of default. In the absence of strong oversight, however, risk-based pricing slides into predatory lending, and a lifeline becomes a trap. Deregulation and new technology have brought credit to many people who had been denied or excluded in the past—but at a high cost. The democratization of credit has, in many ways, become our modern-day safety net, with high interest rates and an array of penalty fees unleashed upon borrowers who make just the slightest slipup, or even no slipup at all.

Policy choices helped get us into this fix, and they will be equally important for getting us out of it. The debt crisis was produced by a collision between an exploitative industry and a vulnerable customer base. The solution will have to include strong action on both fronts. That means policies that point us, on the one hand, toward dramatically higher standards of behavior for the lending industry, and, on the other hand, toward more broadly shared prosperity, with mechanisms of economic opportunity and security that reduce the pressure on Americans to borrow for important life needs.

CURBING ABUSIVE INDUSTRY PRACTICES

"Debt seems to invoke a feeling of hopelessness unlike any other problem I've encountered," explained Ohio consumer Wesley Wannemacher to a full room of senators, congressional staff, industry lobbyists, and consumer advocates at a March 2007 Senate hearing on credit card industry practices. Wannemacher had paid over $6,000 to Chase Bank on a credit card account for which he had made only $3,200 in purchases. He would still be making payments today had Chase not forgiven his debt and issued him a public apology after learning about his plans to testify.[3]

As illuminating as that testimony was, and as gratifying as it was to hear the CEO of a major card issuer publicly apologize to a debtor, most people who have a seemingly endless string of unfair penalty fees and interest rate hikes slapped onto their credit card bills will not get to tell their stories to the Senate. Too many consumers simply continue to pay whatever the lending industry charges.

In August 2006, the U.S. Department of Defense issued a report describing predatory lending practices targeted at active-duty service members and their families. According to the Center for Responsible Lending, payday loans cost military families $80 million in fees each year.[4] An intense effort on the part of military organizations and consumer advocates came to fruition in September 2006: Congress passed a 36 percent interest rate cap on loans to service members and their dependents. Known as the Talent-Nelson Amendment on behalf of its sponsoring senators, the rate cap was tacked onto a military appropriation bill, and won easy approval. Meanwhile, a handful of states have banned payday lending altogether. But in states with minimal consumer protection laws, millions of Americans continue to pay outlandish fees on top of exorbitant interest.

In the summer of 2007, as the subprime mortgage catastrophe widened, federal regulators began to acknowledge the need to tighten lending standards, particularly for hybrid ARM loans, and to encourage financial institutions to work with homeowners facing possible foreclosure. Congress held a series of probing hearings and at this writing seems on the verge of passing legislation.

Even so, an incalculably large number of Americans face the likelihood of losing their homes by one means or another, and the regulatory and legislative fixes may well be too late and too narrowly targeted.[5]

Wesley Wannemacher's testimony, the growing push for credit and pricing reform, the military's tough stand on payday lending, Congress's increased attention to the subprime mortgage debacle—these are encouraging developments. But they exemplify a piecemeal approach that begs the question: Shouldn't *all* borrowers be protected from abusive lending practices? Rather than making policy in response to the most egregious cases that come to light, policymakers should set clear and consistent standards that create a fair lending environment across the board.

This book has documented an array of devastating consequences for borrowers trapped in unfair loans, yet the lending industry is held accountable only in the most extreme and indefensible of instances, like the Providian case in the credit card arena or the kickback scandals of the student loan industry. For all the talk of personal responsibility, there is still a serious dearth of lender responsibility.

It is time for Congress to step in and establish a framework for reform, based on broad principles like responsibility, transparency, and accountability, and backed up by a strong enforcement mechanism. Lenders should be required to gauge borrowers' ability to repay and offer loans on the best terms for which a borrower can qualify; they should provide clear, consistent, and reliable information covering all the key components of a loan; and they should make fair loans that aren't loaded up with tricks and traps. These principles can be applied across an array of loans, from the mortgage market to credit cards. They can and must be enforced by a strong, overarching regulatory authority with the sole mission of consumer protection.

PRINCIPLES OF LENDING-INDUSTRY REFORM

1. Insist on Clear, Consistent, and Reliable Terms

Innovation in the lending industry has become synonymous with highly complex formulas that are not only inscrutable to consumers, but all too often designed to deceive even those borrowers paying in good faith. Loan terms should be clear, consistent, and reliable, whether we're talking about credit cards, mortgages, or installment loans.

Under existing law, several key features must be prominently displayed on all credit card disclosures. But, in practice, one clause supersedes all others: "We reserve the right to change the terms and conditions of the agreement at any time, for any reason." As long as that's the case, everything else—and meaningful competition among products, for that matter—is illusory. Today, the business model of the credit card industry is to aggressively market as many credit cards to as many customers as possible, and then to ensnare people in hair-trigger traps that can increase the cost of credit far beyond what cardholders would reasonably anticipate when they sign up. Disclosures should mean something, and lenders shouldn't have the right to unilaterally change them at any time. In a fair lending environment, there is no room for "any time, any reason" clauses, universal default, or late fees and penalty interest rates that drastically alter the original offer.

Like Al Ynigues, many first-time home buyers find that the

terms of the loan they thought they expected morph into something very different when they sit down at the closing table. The surprises continue when a 2/28 or 3/27 loan resets to a higher interest rate or when a borrower tries to refinance and is slapped with prepayment penalties. Prior to closing, home buyers should have full disclosure of all loan terms and conditions in easily understandable language. If the loan features an adjustable introductory rate, lenders should prominently explain how much a home buyer's payments will increase under a range of circumstances.

Payday lenders claim to offer a one-time fix for a financial pinch, yet their sky-high fees increase the likelihood that their low-income customers will have to roll the loan over again and again. And the majority of payday loan borrowers do. Until the interest rates on these loans are capped—the 36 percent cap for military borrowers seems a reasonable measure to extend to all small loans—borrowers should at least be given clear information about the true costs.

Used-car lots that offer buy here, pay here products snooker low-income car buyers by failing to disclose the prices of the cars they sell. Instead, they back into the price of the car based on what they decide they can get the buyer, often charging far more than the car is worth.[6] While these practices cry out for stronger regulation in a number of areas, an important first step would be to disclose prices to all would-be buyers up front and not make the price a function of the highest dollar amount that the seller can extract in monthly payments from the buyer.

While the details differ, these various types of loans raise common issues. One is the need for a clear, easily understandable, consistent disclosure. The recent GAO study on credit cards found that most contracts were written well above the level at which most Americans read. For disclosure to be meaningful, it must give each borrower an accurate idea of the overall cost of a loan—something like the Minimum Payment Warning bill introduced by Hawaii senator Daniel Akaka, which wants to require credit card companies to disclose with each statement how long it will take and how much in interest and principal a borrower will end up paying by simply sending in the minimum payment each month. That would certainly be a big step forward. And the idea could carry over to some other lending products as well.

While good disclosure is necessary, however, it is far from sufficient. As long as the lending industry loads up its products with tricks and traps and claims the right to apply them at its discretion, the deck is stacked. Congress needs to step in and simply ban unfair practices like universal default and retroactive penalty pricing, while carefully monitoring lending industry practices for new tricks.

2. Risk-Based Pricing That Truly Reflects Risk (and Doesn't Aggravate It)

A common lending industry mantra is that risk-based pricing has opened up credit to those who historically would have found it impossible to get a mortgage or a credit card. Yet risk-based pricing has become an excuse to charge borrowers unreasonable rates and fees, regardless of actual risk. A $39 late fee and a retroactive penalty interest rate of 29.99 percent are surely not risk-based responses to a credit card payment that is a day late. Furthermore, as a number of members of the House Financial Services Committee pointed out in recent congressional hearings, retroactively increasing the interest rate on a credit card balance seems like a good way to actually increase the risk to the lender that the borrower will default, rather than reduce or prospectively recalibrate that risk. This is why regulators should do more to monitor these types of policies and set reasonable limits on penalty pricing.

As 2/28 and 3/27 mortgages proliferated, underwriters generally only assessed the ability of borrowers to repay under introductory teaser rates, even though the monthly payments were going to go sharply higher in two or three years. If lenders cling to the phrase "risk-based pricing," they should also be obliged to do some real risk assessment and not make loans that no objective person would believe a borrower could ever repay.

The challenge is to set and enforce comprehensive and clear standards of fairness across the spectrum of financial services products, so that loans can account for risk without contributing to it.

3. A Neutral Regulatory Body to Set and Enforce Fair Lending Practices

The lending industry has many regulators (some lenders can even choose their own regulator), yet the overarching regulatory structure is horrendously weak. As consumer finance expert and Harvard law professor Elizabeth Warren has argued, consumer product safety laws make it impossible for anyone in the United States to buy a toaster that has a one-in-five chance of bursting into flames, yet there is nothing to stop a consumer from taking out a mortgage with a one-in-five chance of foreclosure.[7]

Without an enforcement entity empowered to regulate the

market on behalf of consumers, fraud and irresponsible lending practices have run rampant. Mortgage brokers wield great power over the lending decisions of borrowers, yet are typically subject only to a few flimsy licensing requirements at the state level. As a result, brokers who come on as the borrower's friend or advocate can use their influence to steer home buyers into loans at higher interest rates than they actually qualify for, pocketing kickbacks along the way.[8] Strong federal standards should be established to protect consumers throughout the mortgage process. Consumers should be steered into the best possible loans for which they qualify, not the worst. Mortgage lenders operate freely across state lines, so their salespeople and brokers ought to be licensed at the federal level—by an agency with the public interest as its first concern.

Something like an Office of Consumer Finance or, as Warren proposes, a Financial Product Safety Commission, is long overdue. Such an agency could closely monitor financial products to ensure that they are safe for consumers. It could set clear guidelines, requiring some features to be prominently disclosed and making sure that other features (such as punitive prepayment fees and universal default clauses) never find their way into a loan in the first place.

PRINCIPLES OF ECONOMIC POLICY REFORM

1. Boosting Savings and Assets

When an economic shock like job loss or a medical emergency hits, credit cards or payday loans often serve as an unforgiving, high-interest safety net. Encouraging and providing incentives for low- and middle-income families to save and build assets can equip people with the financial reserves to weather tough times so that they don't resort to credit card cash advances or the payday lender down the block.

The United States needs a comprehensive savings and asset-building policy. What we have, unfortunately, is a scattershot set of policies that, taken together, largely benefit those households on the higher rungs of the income ladder. As a result, too many families find themselves teetering on the ledge of financial security, often only one paycheck away from disaster. According to the Corporation for Enterprise Development, the federal government spent $367 billion on asset-building policies in 2005, and 45 percent of the money went to households with incomes over $1 million.[9] The largest asset-building expenditure—the home mortgage deduction—is particularly skewed toward the best-off households. The bottom half of American earners receive 2.9 percent of the tax benefits, while the richest 10 percent receive 59 percent.

Policymakers need to consider the overall impact of these savings incentives and begin to construct a system that focuses on low- and middle-income families. For many such families, a modest subsidy could make a significant difference in the ability to get through a financial emergency or make a down payment on a home.

As things stand, credit cards and home equity loans have become, for all too many Americans, the automatic response to an unexpected financial need. To help promote traditional savings, existing tax credits, such as the Savers Credit, should be expanded. That credit, created in 2001 to encourage low-income households to contribute to retirement savings vehicles, could be broadened to cover both nonretirement savings and middle-income households. An alternative to expanding the tax credit would be to establish a universal program, such as the Auto Save system proposed by the New America Foundation.[10] Under that plan, employers making payroll deductions would automatically enroll at a certain contribution rate. Employees would be able to opt out, but participation would be the norm.

America Saves, an existing program, could serve as a model in the mission of building a nation of savers. Managed by the Consumer Federation of America, America Saves involves roughly a thousand nonprofit groups around the country, providing participants with tools as well as information.[11] Participating banks often waive minimum-deposit requirements, and individuals who join the program are offered tailored guidance in setting up a savings account and understanding other mainstream financial services.

In recent years, many credit unions have added small, low-interest loans to the portfolio of products they offer their members. In addition, a growing number of credit unions have been experimenting with products designed to protect their members from high-interest debt. The North Carolina State Employees' Credit Union, after noticing that an alarming number of its members were having checks cashed by payday lenders, created an alternative form of payday loan with a 12 percent interest rate and a requirement that borrowers put 5 percent of the proceeds into a savings account, thus solving a short-term cash crunch and encouraging asset building at the same time.[12] Public policy has a role to play in offering incentives to scale up pilot programs of this sort and gradually make them available to everyone.

Savings and asset-building incentives can also play an important part in boosting homeownership: as the cost of housing has grown and incomes have stagnated, saving enough for an adequate down payment has become a daunting challenge. With many recent home buyers putting zero money down, today's young families are carrying mortgage debt 60 percent higher than their parents did.[13] Ideas like HomeSavers accounts—dedicated matched accounts for low- to middle-income households—could help working Americans save enough to make a substantial down payment, so that a home truly becomes an asset.

While crafting incentives to better assist low- and middle-income households with their saving and asset-building efforts, policymakers must take care not to structure these incentives as a replacement for existing social insurance policies; that was a key defect of the ill-conceived idea to replace Social Security with private accounts. These policies must be a supplement, not a replacement. Social insurance needs to be strengthened, not weakened.

2. Strengthening Economic Opportunity

Being poor is expensive—low-income Americans tend to pay more for a wide range of household necessities from groceries to auto insurance and, of course, loans and other financial services products.[14] Working families trying to earn their way into the middle class—and many families already there—are feeling squeezed, too. After covering the basics, today's typical two-earner family has less money left over than a typical one-earner family had a generation ago.[15] The economic challenges underlying this reality are enormous, and addressing them all will require a sea change in public policy. Nevertheless, there are concrete things we can do in the near term to boost economic and educational opportunity, increase workers' earnings, and strengthen social insurance—all important steps toward that sea change.

3. Reducing Student Debt

One of the defining American values is our belief in equal access to high-quality education. All students willing to work hard at their studies should be able to obtain the skills and training necessary to pursue the careers of their choice. With most middle-class jobs now requiring at least some college education, and with earnings for high school graduates on the decline in recent years, college seems more important than ever. Because of its high cost, however, hundreds of thousands of college-qualified low- and moderate-income students downgrade to community college or forgo higher education altogether. Too many of those who do go to college begin their careers saddled with unmanageable debt. Our financial aid system was founded on the principle of opportunity, yet it often ends up impeding opportunity rather than expanding it.

All students willing to put in the academic work required to pursue and complete a college degree should be given the opportunity to do so without taking on a heavy debt burden. It is reasonable to expect students to borrow a manageable amount for college; after all, they will be the primary beneficiaries of the investment. But the balance between grant and loan aid has shifted way too far, and our policymakers can and should do much more to swing the pendulum back.

Our student aid system is a patchwork of grants, loans, work-study programs, and tax credits, yet the primary way that students pay for college is through loans. Congress needs to review all the existing strands of student aid, simplify and convert them into a single guaranteed package, and provide early notification to families about their available options. (Demos has proposed a Contract for College based on these ideas.)[16] Such a plan would increase college enrollment and completion rates among low- and moderate-income students, lower student debt burdens, and allow families to plan intelligently. Under the Contract for College, for example, a student whose family income is below $25,000 would receive a grant of $9,000 to cover 75 percent of the cost of enrollment at a four-year public college, plus work-study income of $1,500 and a subsidized loan for $1,500. Through a sliding scale, the balance would shift more heavily toward loans for students from higher-income families. A student with household income between $50,000 and $74,999, for example, might receive a grant to cover 55 percent of the cost of enrollment at a four-year public college, with work-study income of $1,500 and a subsidized loan of $3,900.

4. Making Work Pay: Bolstering Earnings

America's middle class was built by a combination of hard work, private-sector commitment, and public policy investment. American workers have held up their end of the bargain, working longer hours than do workers in many other industrialized nations. Meanwhile, the social contract has fallen apart. Far too many Americans work hard without a realistic chance to move up the economic ladder.

Not everyone can go to college, and in fact, we have seen an explosion of low-wage service sector jobs that do not call for higher education and offer little or no opportunity for promotion. Today, able-bodied adults are expected to work, and unemployment rates are low. Finding work isn't the problem. Finding work that provides a path for advancement and a living wage is. Millions of Americans work full-time and still earn too little to meet basic needs. Far more must be done to lift these households out of poverty. In 2007, Congress passed the first increase in the federal minimum wage in ten years, bringing it up to $7.25 per hour. Several states have passed minimum wage hikes through ballot initiatives, indicating widespread public support for policies that reward work.[17] Even the new, long overdue, and hard-won federal minimum leaves many families in poverty or with too wide a gap between wages and the cost of living. Congress should establish a wage floor that truly lifts a full-time worker's family out of poverty, and then index the amount to inflation so that, as the cost of living grows higher, workers' earnings keep pace. To address the gap between earnings and basic expenses, Congress should also significantly expand the Earned Income Tax Credit (EITC), one of the few tax incentives designed to assist low-income workers.

Unions provide workers with a powerful form of leverage; unionized workers typically still enjoy significantly higher earnings and more comprehensive benefits than nonunionized workers. Unions also frequently offer job training that can help members move up the economic ladder. Today, less than 10 percent of private-sector workers are in unions, and the right to unionize is under continual attack.[18] The Employee Free Choice Act, which would require employers to recognize unions when a majority of employees have signed union cards, is a crucial first step. While the House of Representatives passed this legislation in early 2007, as of our writing, the Senate had not yet followed suit, and President Bush was expected to veto the bill if it got that far.[19]

5. Rebuilding the Safety Net
One of the big changes wrought by the new economy is a move away from job stability toward sharply higher volatility and insecurity. Riskier times call for a rethinking of our existing system of unemployment insurance. Under today's system, most workers are ineligible for benefits, and the benefit levels replace only a portion—roughly one-third—of an average worker's earnings. States should examine their programs and modify rules so that more low-wage workers have protection against temporary income loss.

Losing a job has never been easy. Today, unemployment often brings a cascade of economic shocks. Many people lose health insurance as well as income. Even for people who have coverage, a medical emergency can lead to financial trouble. Indeed, a common theme emerges in bankruptcy filings and credit card statements—all too often, medical expenses are a big culprit. There is a growing awareness of the problem of medical debt, particularly as health care costs continue to climb while the ranks of the uninsured expand. Medical debt is a symptom of our broken health care system. As Congress and presidential candidates discuss proposals to reform that system, affordability should have a big place in the discussion. Extending coverage to all would be a monumental achievement, but even many people with health insurance can get hit with huge bills that force them to borrow. Policymakers should carefully consider how much individual cost exposure is appropriate in order to ensure that Americans are protected from high levels of health care debt.

This list of policy prescriptions is illustrative, not exhaustive; we offer it in the spirit of stirring discussion and debate. In America today, debt is a near-universal experience among low- and middle-income families, yet it has been the subject of strikingly little public discussion. Beneath the radar, our debts are tearing us apart, leaving us vulnerable and desperate and evoking the sense of hopelessness described by Wesley Wannemacher in his Senate testimony. It is long past time for our leaders to address this monumental problem, to restore not only our financial health but also the quintessentially American faith in a better future. For that, too, could become a casualty of our debt epidemic.

POLICY AND ADVOCACY ORGANIZATIONS ADDRESSING DEBT/LENDING PRACTICES

ACORN
www.acorn.org
ACORN, the Association of Community Organizations for Reform Now, is the nation's largest community organization of low- and moderate-income families, working together for social justice and stronger communities. Their Web site provides opportunities to take action, volunteer, or join local campaigns.

Americans for Fairness in Lending
www.affil.org
AFFIL is an umbrella group of consumer, civil rights, and other organizations working together to promote commonsense reforms of the lending industry. On its Web site, you can take action by writing your congressperson, sign up for regular alerts about important legislation, find information about common tricks of the lending industry, and link to resources for help managing your debt.

Center for Responsible Lending
www.responsiblelending.org
The Center for Responsible Lending is a nonprofit, nonpartisan research and policy organization dedicated to protecting homeownership and family wealth by working to eliminate abusive financial practices. CRL is affiliated with Self-Help, one of the nation's largest community development financial institutions. Its Web site offers a range of research reports,

policy briefs, and fact sheets on everything from payday loans to sub-prime mortgages.

Consumer Action

www.consumer-action.org

Consumer Action is a national nonprofit education and advocacy organization offering many free services to consumers. Visit its Web site to download its annual credit card survey, which details common credit card industry practices, and to search the Consumer Services Guide for help with questions and problems on a range of consumer issues.

Consumer Federation of America

www.consumerfed.org

CFA is an advocacy, research, education, and service organization comprised of more than three hundred nonprofit organizations located throughout the nation with a combined membership exceeding 50 million people. Its Web site provides information about its work on a range of consumer issues, including recent press releases, policy publications, and links to other consumer resources.

Consumers Union

www.consumersunion.org

Consumers Union (CU) is an expert, independent, nonprofit organization whose mission is to work for a fair, just, and safe marketplace for all consumers. CU publishes *Consumer Reports*. Visit its Web site to get more information on pending legislation to address lending abuses and to take action on a range of lending reforms.

Demos

www.demos.org

Demos is a nonpartisan public policy research and advocacy organization committed to building an America that achieves its highest democratic ideals. Visit the Web site for information on a range of economic issues, including research reports, fact sheets, and policy briefs on a range of debt-related issues.

National Consumer Law Center
www.nclc.org
The National Consumer Law Center (NCLC) is the nation's consumer law expert, helping consumers, their advocates, and public policy makers use powerful and complex consumer laws on behalf of low-income and vulnerable Americans seeking economic justice. Its Web site features information about their legal campaigns and offers a range of legal resources for consumer lawyers.

U.S. PIRG
www.uspirg.org
U.S. Public Interest Research Group serves as the national association and federal lobbying office for state PIRGS, which are nonprofit, nonpartisan advocacy organizations that take on powerful interests on behalf of their one million members nationwide. Recent PIRG financial advocacy campaigns have focused on exposing unfair credit card practices, stopping predatory rent-to-own and payday lenders, solving student loan debt problems, fighting identity theft, and improving the accuracy of credit reports and credit scores.

Woodstock Institute
www.woodstockinst.org
The Woodstock Institute is a leader in mortgage and consumer lending research, documenting industry trends that affect the ability of working households to achieve homeownership and build assets. Visit the Web site for research publications on debt-related topics.

POLICY AND ADVOCACY ORGANIZATIONS ADDRESSING STUDENT DEBT

Campus Progress
www.campusprogress.org
Campus Progress, part of the Center for American Progress, works to help young people—advocates, activists, journalists, artists, and others—make their voices heard on a range of issues, including student debt. Visit

the Web site to learn more about, and join, their Debt Hits Hard campaign, aimed at addressing rising student loan debt.

Project on Student Debt
www.projectonstudentdebt.org
The Project on Student Debt works to increase public understanding of student loan debt trends and the implications for families, the economy, and society. Recognizing that loans play a critical role in making college possible, the Project's goal is to identify cost-effective solutions that expand educational opportunity, protect family financial security, and advance economic competitiveness. Visit the Web site to join its campaign, share your story, and get more information about pending legislation.

State PIRGs Higher Education Project
www.pirg.org/highered
Visit the Web site to join this U.S. PIRG campaign to lower student debt, reduce the costs of textbooks, and reduce subsidies to student loan companies.

United States Student Association
www.usstudents.org
The United States Student Association, the country's oldest and largest national student-led organization, develops current and future leaders and amplifies the student voice at the local, state, and national levels by mobilizing grassroots power to win concrete victories on student issues. Visit the Web site to learn more about its campaigns and become a member.

GENERAL PERSONAL FINANCE RESOURCES

Bankrate, Inc.
www.bankrate.com
This site offers an array of information about financial products from credit cards to mortgages. Bankrate also features monthly articles addressing some of the most common personal finance issues.

Finaid.org
www.finaid.org
This site offers comprehensive information and tools to help compare and select student loans.

To Find a Credit Counselor
National Foundation for Credit Counseling
www.nfcc.org
The National Foundation for Credit Counseling (NFCC) consists of more than a hundred member agencies and more than nine hundred local offices throughout the country. The NFCC can help you find an accredited credit counseling agency in your area. The Web site also provides a range of general budgeting and debt advice.

To Find a Lawyer
National Association of Consumer Advocates (NACA)
www.naca.net/find-consumer-protection-attorneys
The National Association of Consumer Advocates (NACA) is a nationwide organization of more than a thousand attorneys who represent and have represented hundreds of thousands of consumers victimized by fraudulent, abusive, and predatory business practices.

To Find a Housing Counselor
Department of Housing and Urban Development
www.hud.gov/offices/hsg/sfh/hcc/hcs.cfm
The Department of Housing and Urban Development sponsors housing counseling agencies throughout the country that can provide advice on buying a home, renting, defaults, foreclosures, credit issues, and reverse mortgages.

NOTES

FOREWORD

1. Mortgage data from Elizabeth Warren, "The Middle Class on the Precipice: Rising Financial Risks for American Families," *Harvard Magazine*, January/February 2006. Credit card data from Cardweb .com, "Card Debt," November 22, 2004, http://www.cardweb.com/ cardtrak/news/2004/november/22a.html.

2. Center for Responsible Lending, "Predatory Payday Lending Traps Borrowers," Factsheet, 2005, http://www.responsiblelending.org/ pdfs/2b002-payday2005.pdf.

1: BORROWING TO MAKE ENDS MEET

1. "Don't Buy Stuff You Can't Afford," aired on NBC's *Saturday Night Live*, February 4, 2006.

2. Jessica Bennett, "Spend Cycle," *Newsweek*, August 9, 2006.

3. Elizabeth Warren and Amelia Warren Tyagi, "Digging Out of Debt," *Orlando Sentinel*, February 15, 2004.

4. Cindy Zeldin and Mark Rukavina, *Borrowing to Stay Healthy: How Credit Card Debt Is Related to Medical Expense*, Demos and the Access Project, January 2007.

5. Project on Student Debt, "High Hopes, Big Debts," June 2006, http://www.projectonstudentdebt.org/.

6. Lawrence Gladieux and Laura Perna, "Borrowers Who Drop Out: A Neglected Aspect of the College Student Loan Trend," National Center for Public Policy and Higher Education, May 2005, http://www.highereducation.org/reports/borrowing/index.shtml.

7. Smith College, "College Students Use Credit Cards to Pay for Their Education," news release, August 17, 2005, http://www

.smith.edu/newsoffice/releases/05-007.html; U.S. Government Accountability Office, *College Textbooks: Enhanced Offerings Appear to Drive Recent Price Increases*, Report to Congressional Requests, GAO-05-806, July 29, 2005, http://www.gao.gov/new.items/d05806.pdf.

8. Elizabeth Warren, "The Middle Class on the Precipice: Rising Financial Risks for American Families," *Harvard Magazine*, January/February 2006.

9. Lawrence Mishel, Jared Bernstein, and Sylvia Allegretto, *The State of Working America 2006/2007* (Ithaca, NY: Cornell University Press, 2007).

10. "Credit Cards: They Really *Are* Out to Get You," *Consumer Reports*, November 2005.

11. Director's statement on the *Maxed Out* Web site, http://www.maxedoutmovie.com/director/index.html.

12. Louis Uchitelle, *The Disposable American: Layoffs and Their Consequences* (New York: Knopf, 2006), p. 36.

13. Ibid., p. 38.

14. Robert D. Manning, *Credit Card Nation: The Consequences of America's Addiction to Credit* (New York: Basic Books, 2000), p. 37.

15. Ibid., p. 38, based on Federal Reserve data.

16. Lawrence Mishel, Jared Bernstein, and Sylvia Allegretto, *The State of Working America 2004/2005* (Ithaca, NY: Cornell University Press, 2005), p. 149.

17. Julie Appleby and Sharon Silke Carty, "Ailing GM Looks to Scale Back Generous Health Benefits," *USA Today*, June 23, 2005.

18. David J. Ginzi, "Job Layoffs—A Festering National Crisis?" *Commercial Lending Review*, November/December 2006.

19. Uchitelle, *Disposable American*, chap. 6.

20. Michel, Bernstein, and Allegretto, *State of Working America 2004/2005*, p. 150.

21. CNN exit polls data, http://www.cnn.com/ELECTION/2006/pages/results/states/US/H/00/epolls.0.html.

22. Mishel, Bernstein, and Allegretto, *State of Working America 2006/2007*.

23. Tamara Draut, *Strapped: Why America's 20- and 30-Somethings Can't Get Ahead* (New York: Doubleday, 2006), chap. 1.

24. Michael J. Mandel, "College: The Payoff Shrinks," *BusinessWeek*, September 12, 2005.

25. Mishel, Bernstein, and Allegretto, *State of Working America 2004/2005*, p. 62.

26. Aaron Bernstein, "Waking Up from the American Dream," *Business-Week*, December 1, 2003.

27. Warren, "Middle Class on the Precipice."

28. Elizabeth Warren and Amelia Warren Tyagi, *The Two-Income Trap: Why Middle Class Mothers and Fathers Are Going Broke* (New York: Basic Books, 2003), pp. 51–52.

29. Jacob S. Hacker, *The Great Risk Shift: The Assault on American Jobs, Families, Health Care, and Retirement* (New York: Oxford University Press, 2006), pp. 27–32.

30. Howard Karger, *Shortchanged: Life and Debt in the Fringe Economy* (San Francisco: Berrett-Koehler, 2005).

31. Demos and the Center for Responsible Lending, *The Plastic Safety Net: The Reality Behind Debt in America*, October 2005, p. 19.

32. Zeldin and Rukavina, *Borrowing to Stay Healthy*.

33. Robert Manning, *Credit Cards on Campus: Costs and Consequences of Student Debt*, Consumer Federation of America, June 1999.

34. Demos and the Center for Responsible Lending, *Plastic Safety Net*, p. 13.

35. Ibid., p. 19.

36. Alison Cassady and Edmund Mierzwinski, *Mistakes Do Happen: A Look at Errors in Consumer Credit Reports*, National Association of State PIRGS, 2004, http://www.uspirg.org.

37. Kathy Chu, "How to Escape Card Debt," *USA Today*, December 15, 2006.

38. Elizabeth Warren, "Show Me the Money," *New York Times*, October 24, 2005.

39. Demos, *A House of Cards: Refinancing the American Dream*, Winter 2007.

40. Alyssa Katz, "Prime Suspect," *Mother Jones*, September/October 2006.

41. Ellen Schloemer, Wei Li, Keith Ernst, and Kathleen Keest, *Losing Ground: Foreclosures in the Subprime Market and Their Cost to Homeowners*, Center for Responsible Lending, December 2006, http://www.responsiblelending.org.

2: AN INDUSTRY RUN AMOK

1. Paul Rizzo, "Car-Title Loans, Payday Loans Leave Virginia Consumers Strapped for Cash," *Payday Loan Times*, July 31, 2006, http://www.paydayloantimes.com.

2. Jeffrey Williams, "Pedagogy of Debt," *College Literature*, September 22, 2006; also interview by James Lardner, July 2007.

3. Tony Pugh, "Predatory Lending Victims Tell Senators Tales of Exploitation," *Miami Herald*, July 27, 2002.

4. Kris James Mitchener, "Bank Supervision, Regulation, and Instability During the Great Depression," NBER Working Paper No. W10475, May 2004, http://ssrn.com/abstract=541701.

5. Federal Deposit Insurance Corporation, *A Brief History of Deposit Insurance in the United States* (Washington, DC: FDIC, 1998).

6. Jill M. Hendrickson, "The Long and Bumpy Road to Glass-Steagall Reform: A Historical and Evolutionary Analysis of Banking Legislation," *American Journal of Economics and Sociology* 60, no. 4 (October 2001).

7. "Deregulated," *Consumer Reports*, July 2002.

8. Nicholas Lemann, "Change in the Banks," *The Atlantic*, August 1985.

9. Senate Business and Commerce, "Interim Report: Usury Laws and Credit Counseling," interim report to the 79th Texas Legislature 2003.

10. Lemann, "Change in the Banks."

11. R.A. Gilbert, "Requiem for Regulation Q: What It Did and Why It Passed," *Federal Reserve Bank of St. Louis Review*, February 1986.

12. Jonathan R. Macey, "The False Promise of Deregulation in Banking," Yale Law School research paper, 2005.

13. Ibid.

14. T. Curry and L. Shibut, "The Cost of the Savings and Loan Crisis: Truth and Consequences," *FDIC Banking Review* 13, no. 2 (2000), pp. 26–35.

15. *Marquette Nat. Bank v. First of Omaha Corp.*, 439 U.S. 299 (1978).

16. Robin Stein, "The Ascendancy of the Credit Card Industry," *Frontline: Secret History of the Credit Card*, November 23, 2004.

17. James M. Ackerman, "Interest Rates and the Law: A History of Usury," *Arizona State Law Journal* 61 (1981).

18. House Financial Services Committee, "Cutting Through the Red Tape: Regulatory Relief for America's Community-Based Banks," testimony of John Reich, May 12, 2004.

19. Kenneth D. Jones and Timothy S. Critchfield, "Consolidation in the U.S. Banking Industry: Is the Long, Strange Trip About to End?" *FDIC Banking Review* 17 (February 4, 2005).

20. Ronald J. Mann, *Charging Ahead: The Growth and Regulation of Payment Card Markets* (New York: Cambridge University Press, 2006).

21. J. Alfred Broaddus Jr., "The Bank Merger Wave: Causes and Consequences," speech to the Henrico Business Council of Richmond, VA, September 17, 1998, http://www.richmondfed.org.

22. Jones and Critchfield, "Consolidation in the U.S. Banking Industry."

23. James Campen, "Neighborhoods, Banks, and Capital Flows: The Transformation of the U.S. Financial System and the Community Reinvestment Movement," *Review of Radical Political Economics* 30, no. 4 (1998).

24. Dan Immergluck and Geoff Smith, "Bigger, Faster . . . But Better? How Changes in the Financial Services Industry Affect Small Business Lending in Urban Areas," paper prepared for the Brookings Center on Urban and Metropolitan Policy, September 2001.

25. J.J. Xiao, L. Malroutu, and G.I. Olson, "The Impact of Banking Deregulation on Family Checking Ownership and Balances," *Family Economics and Resource Management Biennial*, 1995.

26. Cardweb.com, "Late Fee Bug," May 17, 2002, http://www.cardweb.com/cardtrak/news/2002/may/17a.html.

27. U.S. Public Interest Research Group, "The Credit Card Trap: How to Spot It, How to Avoid It," April 2001, http://www.uspirg.org.

28. U.S. Government Accountability Office, *Credit Cards: Increased Complexity in Rates and Fees Heightens Need for More Effective Disclosures to Consumers*, Report to the Ranking Minority Member, Permanent Subcommittee on Investigations, Committee on Homeland Security and Governmental Affairs, U.S. Senate, GAO-06-929, September 2006, http://www.gao.gov/.

29. Cardweb.com, "Fee Escalation," June 18, 2003, http://www.card web.com/cardtrak/news/2003/june/18a.html.

30. Cardweb.com, "Fee Revenues," July 9, 1999, http://www.cardweb .com/cardtrak/news/1999/july/8a.html.

31. Office of the Comptroller of the Currency, "Providian to Cease Unfair Practices, Pay Consumers Minimum of $300 million Under Settlement with OCC and San Francisco District Attorney," news release, June 28, 2000.

32. Samuel Issacharoff and Erin F. Delaney, "Credit Card Accountability," *University of Chicago Law Review* 73, no. 1 (Winter 2006).

33. Robert Salladay, "Credit Card Debt Warnings Rejected," *San Francisco Chronicle*, December 24, 2002.

34. Federal Reserve, "Federal Funds Rate, Historical Data," April 28, 2003, http://www.federalreserve.gov.

35. U.S. Census Bureau, *Statistical Abstract of the United States 2002* (Washington, DC: U.S. Census Bureau, 2003).

36. "Largest Banks: 2003," *American Banker*, http://www.american banker.com/.

37. Federal Reserve Bank G.20 and G.19; U.S. Senate Committee on Banking, Housing, and Urban Affairs, "Examining the Billing, Marketing, and Disclosure Practices of the Credit Card Industry, and Their Impact on Consumers," testimony of Elizabeth Warren, January 25, 2007.

38. Lemann, "Change in the Banks."

39. Sandra E. Black and Donald P. Morgan, "Risk and the Democratization of Credit Cards," Research Paper 9815, Federal Reserve Bank of New York, 1998.

40. Campen, "Neighborhoods, Banks, and Capital Flows."
41. Debbie G. Bocian, Keith S. Ernst, and Wei Li, *Unfair Lending: The Effect of Race and Ethnicity on the Price of Subprime Mortgages*, Center for Responsible Lending, May 31, 2006.
42. U.S. Senate Committee on Banking, Housing, and Urban Affairs, "The Importance of Financial Literacy Among College Students," testimony of Robert D. Manning, September 5, 2002.
43. Randall S. Kroszner, "The Economics and Politics of Financial Modernization," *Economic Policy Review* 6, no. 4 (October 2000).
44. Ronald J. Mann, "Bankruptcy Reform and the 'Sweat Box' of Credit Card Debt," *University of Illinois Law Review*, no. 1 (2007).
45. Christine Blair and Rose M. Kushmeider, "Challenges to the Dual Banking System: The Funding of Bank Supervision," FDIC Banking Review Series 2006, vol. 18-1, http://www.fdic.gov/.
46. "Credit Cards: They Really *Are* Out to Get You," *Consumer Reports*, November 2005.
47. Issacharoff and Delaney, "Credit Card Accountability."
48. Jonathan Brown, *Financial Deregulation: The Need for Safeguards* (Washington, DC: Essential Information Inc., 1993).
49. Howard Karger, *Shortchanged: Life and Debt in the Fringe Economy* (San Francisco: Berrett-Koehler, 2005); Kim Leonard, "State Sues 'Payday' Lender," *Pittsburgh Tribune Review*, September 28, 2006.

3: GOTCHA!

1. Nilson Report, "Credit Cards—Holders, Numbers, Spending, and Debt," reported in *1998 Statistical Abstract of the United States* (Washington, DC: U.S. Government Printing Office, 1999), p. 523, table 822.
2. U.S. Government Accountability Office (GAO), *Credit Cards: Increased Complexity in Rates and Fees Heightens Need for More Effective Disclosures to Consumers*, Report to the Ranking Minority Member, Permanent Subcommittee on Investigations, Committee on Homeland Security and Governmental Affairs, U.S. Senate, GAO-06-929, September 2006, p. 1, http://www.gao.gov/; José Gar-

cía, *Borrowing to Make Ends Meet: National Statistics and Trends in Credit Card Debt, 2007 Update*, Demos, 2007.

3. José García, *Borrowing to Make Ends Meet; National Statistics and Trends in Credit Card Debt by Race and Age, 2007 Update*, Demos, 2007.

4. Demos and the Center for Responsible Lending, *The Plastic Safety Net: The Reality Behind Debt in America*, 2005, p. 7.

5. Ibid., p. 1.

6. Robert Gordon and Derek Douglas, "Taking Charge: Attention Credit-Card Companies: When We Want You to Charge Us Hidden Fees, We'll Let You Know," *Washington Monthly*, December 1, 2005.

7. Lewis Mandell, *The Credit Card Industry: A History* (Boston: Twayne Publishers, 1990); Lawrence M. Ausubel, "Book Review: *The Credit Card Industry*, by Lewis Mandell," *Journal of Economic Literature* 30, no. 3. (September 1992), pp. 1517–18.

8. Matty Simmons, *The Credit Card Catastrophe: The 20th Century Phenomenon That Changed the World* (New York: Barricade Books, 1995), p. 30.

9. GAO, *Credit Cards*, p. 9.

10. No more, of course. In the early 1980s, Bank of America began acquiring banks in other states, until in 1998 it was itself acquired by NationsBank; the combined entity, which retained the Bank of America name, promptly embarked on another run of acquisitions, culminating with MBNA in 2005. Today it is the biggest credit card issuer in the world, and the biggest consumer and small-business bank in the United States.

11. MasterCard Worldwide, "Frequently Asked Questions," http://www.mastercard.com/us/company/en/docs/MasterCard%20FAQ.pdf.

12. Teresa A. Sullivan, Elizabeth Warren, and Jay Westbrook, *The Fragile Middle Class: Americans in Debt* (New Haven, CT: Yale University Press, 2001); Robin Stein, "The Ascendancy of the Credit-Card Industry," *Frontline: Secret History of the Credit Card*, November 23, 2004.

13. Stein, "Ascendancy of the Credit Card Industry."

14. U.S. General Accounting Office, *U.S. Credit Card Industry: Competitive Developments Need to Be Closely Monitored*, Report to Congressional Requesters, GAO/GGD-94-23, April 1994, http://www.gao.gov.

15. Stein, "Ascendancy of the Credit Card Industry."

16. Ibid.; Jerry Hines, "Delight Makes the Difference: The Story of the AT&T Universal Card," *TQM Magazine* 7, no. 3 (1995), pp. 6–11; Dennis W. Carlton and Alan S. Frankel, "The Antitrust Economics of Credit Card Networks," *Antitrust Law Journal* 63, no. 2 (1995), p. 643.

17. Stein, "Ascendancy of the Credit Card Industry."

18. Ibid.

19. Cardweb.com, "Card Rates," March 19, 2007, http://www.cardweb.com/cardtrak/news/2007/march/19a.html.

20. Stein, "Ascendancy of the Credit Card Industry."

21. Saul Hansell, "Merchants of Debt," *New York Times*, July 2, 1995; Anne M. Petersen, "Lawsuits and Complaints Dog Credit Card Provider," Associated Press, June 1, 1999.

22. Sam Zuckerman, "How Providian Misled Card Holders," *San Francisco Chronicle*, May 5, 2002.

23. Ibid.

24. "Providian Memos Show Sinister Side to Company Founder," Associated Press, May 5, 2002.

25. Zuckerman, "How Providian Misled Card Holders."

26. National Consumer Law Center and Consumer Federation, *Tax Preparers Peddle High-Priced Tax Refund Loans: Millions Skimmed from the Working Poor and the U.S. Treasury*, January 2002.

27. U.S. Senate Committee on Banking, Housing, and Urban Affairs, "Examining the Billing, Marketing, and Disclosure Practices of the Credit Card Industry," testimony of Robert D. Manning, January 25, 2007.

28. Ibid.

29. Mark Huffman, "Minimum Credit Card Payments Going Up, But How Much?" Consumer Affairs, December 19, 2005, http://www.consumeraffairs.com.

30. GAO, *Credit Cards.*
31. Cardweb.com, "Fee Party," January 13, 2005, http://www.card web.com/cardtrak/news/2005/january/13a.html.
32. Consumer Action, "Credit Cards: What You Need to Know," http://www.consumer-action.org/english/articles/credit_cards _what_you_need_to_know/#Topic_05; GAO, *Credit Cards.*
33. CardRatings.com, "Credit Card Cash Advance Pitfalls," *Young Money,* http://www.youngmoney.com.
34. Consumer Action, "Credit Cards: What You Need to Know"; GAO, *Credit Cards,* p. 23.
35. Ibid., pp. 23–25.
36. GAO, *Credit Cards,* p. 24.
37. Consumer Action, "Credit Card Survey 2007," Spring 2007, http://www.consumer-action.org.
38. Gordon and Douglas, "Taking Charge."
39. Zuckerman, "How Providian Misled Card Holders."
40. Ibid.
41. See UnfairCreditCardFees.com; Charles Lee, "Corporate Thievery," *University of Virginia Cavalier Daily,* January 22, 2007.
42. U.S. Senate Committee on Banking, Housing, and Urban Affairs, "Examining the Billing, Marketing, and Disclosure Practices of the Credit Card Industry," testimony of Travis Plunkett, January 25, 2007; Ellen Cannon, "Credit Card Issuers' Profits Grew," Bankrate.com, January 9, 2007, http://www.bankrate.com.
43. Citigroup 2006 SEC Filings, Form 10-K, pp. 22, 26, http://www.citi group.com/citigroup/fin/data/k06c.pdf.
44. U.S. Senate Committee on Banking, Housing, and Urban Affairs, "Examining the Billing, Marketing, and Disclosure Practices of the Credit Card Industry," testimony of Elizabeth Warren, January 25, 2007, p. 4.
45. GAO, *Credit Cards,* p. 6.
46. Oren Bar-Gill, "Seduction by Plastic," *Northwestern University Law Review* 98, no. 4 (2004), pp. 1373–434.
47. Ronald J. Mann, *Charging Ahead: The Growth and Regulation of Payment Card Markets* (New York: Cambridge University Press, 2006).

48. Bar-Gill, "Seduction by Plastic."
49. Cardweb.com, "Orvis Card," January 21, 2007, http://www.card web.com/cardtrak/news/2007/february/21a.html.
50. Miriam Jordan, "Bank of America Casts Wider Net for Hispanics," *Wall Street Journal*, February 13, 2007.
51. Aaron Johnson, "Chase Hocks Credit Cards with Help of Bike Cabs," BankNet 360, October 23, 2006, http://www.banknet360.com/.
52. Ibid.
53. Robert Manning, "Credit Cards on Campus," New American Dream, n.d., http://www.newdream.org/newsletter/creditcards.php.
54. Ray Brady, "Students Hooked on Credit," CBS News, May 3, 2000.
55. Taylor Loyal, "Don't Leave Home Without It," *Mother Jones*, March/April 2002.
56. Nellie Mae Corporation, "Undergraduate Students and Credit Cards: An Analysis of Usage Rates and Trends," May 2005, http://www.nelliemae.com/pdf/ccstudy_2005.pdf.
57. Ibid.
58. Visa Buxx announcement, http://usa.visa.com/personal/cards/prepaid/visa_buxx.html.
59. Caroline E. Mayer, "Girls Go from Hello Kitty to Hello Debit Card: Brand's Power Tapped to Reach Youth," *Washington Post*, October 3, 2004.
60. Ibid.

4: MORTGAGE MAYHEM

1. Alfonso Ynigues interview by José García, June 25, 2007; also U.S. Senate Committee on Banking, Housing and Urban Affairs, "Mortgage Market Turmoil: Causes and Consequences," testimony of Alfonso Ynigues, March 22, 2007.
2. Ibid.
3. Nicholas Lemann, "The Myth of Community Development," *New York Times Magazine*, January 2, 1994.
4. Michael Collins, *Pursuing the American Dream: Homeownership and the Role of Federal Housing Policy*, Millennial Housing Commission, March 2002, p. 31, http://www.nw.org/network/pubs/studies/. For a

summary of the Fair Housing and Equal Credit Opportunity Acts, see http://www.usdoj.gov/crt/housing/housing_coverage.htm; Community Reinvestment Act described at http://www.federalreserve.gov/dcca/cra/; Home Mortgage Disclosure Act at http://www.ffiec.gov/hmda/.

5. Alternate Mortgage Transaction Parity Act, part of Depository Institutions Act of 192, Title VIII, 12 U.S.C. §3800, Pub. L. 97-320, 96 Stat. 1469 (October 15, 1982); Kerry Cooper and Donald R. Fraser, *Banking Deregulation and the New Competition in Financial Service* (Cambridge, MA: Ballinger, 1984); Deborah Goldstein, *Understanding Predatory Lending: Moving Towards a Common Definition and Workable Solutions*, Joint Center for Housing Studies of Harvard University and Neighborhood Reinvestment Corporation, September 1999, p. 22.

6. House Financial Services Committee, Subcommittee on Financial Institutions and Consumer Credit, "Role of the Secondary Market in Subprime Mortgage Lending," opening statement by Carolyn Maloney, May 8, 2007; MortgageInvestment.com, FICO credit scoring, http://www.mortgage-investments.com/Credit_reports/fico_credit_scoring.htm; Andrea Heuson, Wayne Passmore, and Roger Sparks, "Credit Scoring and Mortgage Securitization: Implications for Mortgage Rates and Credit Availability," Finance and Economics Discussion Series, 2000-44, Federal Reserve Board, December 21, 2000, http:///www.federalreserve.gov/.

7. U.S. Senate Committee on Banking, Housing and Urban Affairs, Subcommittee on Housing, Transportation, and Community Development, "Ending Mortgage Abuse: Safeguarding Homebuyers," testimony of Michael D. Calhoun, Center for Responsible Lending, June 26, 2007.

8. Justin Fox, "Subprime's Silver Lining," *Time*, March 22, 2007; *Curious Capitalist* 169, no. 14 (April 2, 2007), p. 53.

9. Ynigues testimony.

10. Ellen Schloemer, Wei Li, Keith Ernst, and Kathleen Keest, *Losing Ground: Foreclosures in the Subprime Market and Their Cost to Home-*

owners, Center for Responsible Lending, December 2006, http://www.responsiblelending.org.

11. Mark Whitehouse, " 'Subprime' Aftermath: Losing the Family Home," *Wall Street Journal*, May 30, 2007.

12. U.S. Senate Committee on Banking, Housing, and Urban Affairs, "Mortgage Market Turmoil," testimony of Alan M. White, March 22, 2007.

13. Center for Responsible Lending, "Subprime Lending Is a Net Drain on Homeownership," CRL Issue Paper No. 14, March 27, 2007, http://www.responsiblelending.org/pdfs/Net-Drain-in-Home-Ownership.pdf.

14. Jonathan Peterson, "Weighing Restraints on Loans," *Los Angeles Times*, February 24, 2007.

15. Seth Lubove and Daniel Taub, "Subprime Fiasco Exposes Manipulation by Mortgage Brokerages," Bloomberg.com, May 30, 2007.

16. Mary Kane, "Commentary," Newhouse News Service, March 16, 2007.

17. Kimberly Blanton. "Dark Side of Subprime Loans," *Boston Globe*, August 3, 2005.

18. Mike Hudson and E. Scott Reckard, "More Homeowners with Good Credit Getting Stuck with Higher-Rate Loans," *Los Angeles Times*, October 24, 2005, http://www.kristinstolte.com/trends_latimes 051024.html.

19. Ren S. Essene and William Apgar, *Understanding Mortgage Market Behavior: Creating Good Mortgage Options for All Americans*, Joint Center for Housing Studies, Harvard University, April 25, 2007.

20. Stacey Myers, "Subprime Lending Practices Under Fire," *Cape Cod Times*, March 18, 2007.

21. Calvin Bradford, "Risk or Race: Racial Disparities and the Subprime Refinance Market," Center for Community Change, 2002, pp. 6–7; Essene and Apgar, "Understanding Mortgage Market Behavior."

22. Ynigues testimony.

23. Ibid.

24. House Financial Services Committee, "Possible Responses to Rising

Mortgage Foreclosures," testimony of David Berenbaum, April 17, 2007.

25. Elizabeth Warren, "Unsafe at Any Rate," *Democracy: A Journal of Ideas*, no. 5 (Summer 2007).

26. James R. Hagerty, "Payment Woes Worsen on Riskiest Mortgages," *Wall Street Journal*, April 4, 2007.

27. Mark Trumbull, "Foreclosure's Shadow Falls Across Diverse Set of U.S. Homeowners," *Christian Science Monitor*, April 9, 2007.

28. U.S. Senate Banking, Housing and Urban Affairs Committee, "Mortgage Market Turmoil," testimony of Irv Ackelsberg, March 22, 2007.

29. Michael Hudson, "How Wall Street Stoked the Mortgage Meltdown," *Wall Street Journal*, June 27, 2007.

30. Robert B. Avery, Raphael W. Bostic, Paul S. Calem, and Glenn B. Canner, "Credit Risk, Credit Scoring, and the Performance of Home Mortgages," *Federal Reserve Bulletin*, July 1996.

31. U.S. Senate Banking, Housing and Urban Affairs Committee, "Mortgage Market Turmoil," statement of Senator Christopher J. Dodd, March 22, 2007.

32. James R. Hagerty, Ruth Simon, Michael Corkery, and Gregory Zuckerman, "At a Mortgage Lender, Rapid Rise, Faster Fall," *Wall Street Journal*, March 13, 2007.

33. Ibid.; Jonathan Lansner, "Take a Test on Mortgage Mess," *Orange County Register*, April 4, 2007.

34. Hagerty, Simon, Corkery, and Zuckerman, "At a Mortgage Lender."

35. Lubove and Taub, "Subprime Fiasco."

36. Ibid.

37. Elizabeth Renuart, "An Overview of the Predatory Lending Process," *Housing Policy Debate* 15, no. 3 (2004).

38. Essene and Apgar, "Understanding Mortgage Market Behavior."

39. Kellie Kim-Sung and Sharon Hermanson, "Experiences of Older Refinance Mortgage Loan Borrowers," AARP Public Policy Institute, January 2003, http://www.aarp.org.

40. Lubove and Taub, "Subprime Fiasco."

41. Ibid.

42. Michele Derus, "Loans Sinking Borrowers, Lenders," *Milwaukee Journal Sentinel*, March 17, 2007.

43. E. Scott Reckard and Mike Hudson, "More Mortgage Lenders Targeted," *Los Angeles Times*, January 31, 2006.

44. House Committee on Oversight and Government Reform, "Foreclosure, Predatory Mortgage and Payday Lending in America's Cities," testimony of Josh Nassar, Center for Responsible Lending, March 21, 2007.

45. Heather Haddon, "Ripple Effects Just Starting to Show," *Passaic County Herald News*, April 10, 2007.

46. Vikas Baja, "A Cross-Country Blame Game," *New York Times*, May 8, 2007; Jim Freer, "Subprime Fallout Hits," *South Florida Business Journal*, April 2, 2007; Kathleen Lynn, "Exotic Loans Carry Big Risks," *The Record* (Hackensack, NJ), December 17, 2006; Andy LaPerriere, "Mortgage Meltdown," *Wall Street Journal*, March 21, 2007.

47. Julie Sturgeon, "Don't Take Your Prime Credit to a Subprime Lender," Bankrate.com, November 1, 2005, http://www.bankrate.com/brm/news/debt/debtcreditguide/main-bank1.asp.

48. Mara Der Hovanesian, Peter Coy, and Matthew Goldstein with David Henry, "Making Sense of the Mortgage Mess," *BusinessWeek*, March 26, 2007.

49. Reckard and Hudson, "More Mortgage Lenders Targeted."

50. John Gittelsohn and Matthew Padilla, "Cutting-Edge Company Becomes a Cautionary Tale," *Orange County Register*, April 30, 2007.

51. Jim Buchta, "Mortgage Brokers Are Closing Shop," *Minneapolis Star Tribune*, July 7, 2007.

52. Julie Creswell, "After Losses, UBS Ousts Its Chief," *New York Times*, July 6, 2007.

53. Ibid.

54. Michael Liedtke, "Wells Fargo Cutting 500 Jobs in Subprime Mortgage Division," Associated Press, March 20, 2007.

55. Chris Isidore, "Subprime Woes Bite General Motors," CNN Money.com, May 3, 2007, http://money.cnn.com/2007/05/03/news/companies/gm_earnings/index.htm.

56. "Separate and Unequal: The Effects of Overcharging by Citigroup,"

Community Reinvestment Act of North Carolina, http://www .cra-nc.org/; Hudson and Reckard, "More Homeowners with Good Credit."

57. Federal Trade Commission, "Citigroup Settles FTC Charges Against the Associates: Record-Setting $215 Million for Subprime Lending Victims," news release, September 19, 2002.

58. Mary Kane, "Poor People, Not Wall Street, Victimized," *Newark Star-Ledger*, March 18, 2007.

59. Carrick Mollenkamp, "HSBC Cleans House at Mortgage Subsidiary; New Boss Named at U.S. Division," *Globe and Mail*, February 23, 2007.

60. Daniel Gross, "Please Do Not Feed Bear," *Slate*, July 3, 2007, http://www.slate.com/id/2169759/.

61. Greg Hitt and James R. Hagerty, "Regulators Are Pressed to Take Tougher Stand on Mortgages," *Wall Street Journal*, March 23, 2007; Sue Kirchhoff, "Regulators: Oversight of Subprime Mortgages Is Lax," *USA Today*, March 22, 2007.

62. Schloemer et al., *Losing Ground*.

63. Fox, "Subprime's Silver Lining."

64. Bob Rayner, "Regulation Isn't the Key to Ownership," *Richmond Times-Dispatch*, March 21, 2007.

65. Chris Arnold, "New Century's Borrowers Worry for Homes," aired on NPR's *All Things Considered*, March 16, 2007.

66. U.S. Census Bureau, "New Residential Sales," historical tables at http://www.census.gov.

67. Robert Kuttner, "The Housing Squeeze," *Boston Globe*, April 7, 2007.

68. Erick Eckholm, "Foreclosures Force Suburbs to Fight Blight," *New York Times*, March 23 2007.

69. Whitehouse, " 'Subprime' Aftermath."

70. Haddon, "Ripple Effects."

71. Mary Kane, "Cities Started to Feel the Pain," *Newark Star-Ledger*, March 18, 2007.

72. Kane, "Commentary"; Eckholm, "Foreclosures Force Suburbs."

73. Haddon, "Ripple Effects"; Almas Sayeed, *From Boom to Bust: Helping Families Prepare for the Rise in Subprime Mortgage Foreclosures*, Cen-

ter for American Progress, March 12, 2007, http://www.american progress.org.

74. Whitehouse, " 'Subprime' Aftermath."

75. Eric S. Belsky, Michael Schill, and Anthony Yezer, *The Effect of the Community Reinvestment Act on Bank and Thrift Home Purchase Mortgage Lending*, Joint Center for Housing Studies, Harvard University, August 2001.

76. Joint Center for Housing Studies, *The State of the Nation's Housing: 2007*, Harvard University, June 26, 2007.

77. LaPerriere, "Mortgage Meltdown."

78. Center for Responsible Lending, "Subprime Lending Is a Net Drain."

5: ASLEEP AT THE SWITCH

1. Seth Lubove and Daniel Taub, "Subprime Fiasco Exposes Manipulation by Mortgage Brokerages," Bloomberg.com, May 30, 2007.

2. Norma Paz-Garcia, "The Hard Sell: Combating Home Equity Lending Fraud in California," Consumers Union, July 1998.

3. Allen J. Fishbein and Patrick Woodall, *Exotic or Toxic? An Examination of the Non-Traditional Mortgage Market for Consumers and Lenders*, Consumer Federation of America, May 2006, p. 1.

4. U.S. Senate Banking, Housing and Urban Affairs Committee, "Mortgage Market Turmoil," testimony of Sandra L. Thompson, director, Division of Supervision and Consumer Protection, Federal Deposit Insurance Corporation, March 22, 2007.

5. Ibid.; Vikas Bajaj, "More Trouble in Subprime Mortgages," *New York Times*, June 15, 2007.

6. U.S.C. Section 1639(1)(2).

7. U.S. Senate Banking, Housing and Urban Affairs Committee, "Mortgage Market Turmoil," statement of Senator Christopher J. Dodd, March 22, 2007.

8. House Banking Committee, "Predatory Lending Practices," testimony of Representative James Leach, May 24, 2000.

9. Craig Torres and Alison Vekshin, "Regulators Criticized for Subprime Loan Problems," Bloomberg.com, March 18, 2007.

10. Dodd, statement.

11. Grep Ip, "Regulators Scrutinized in Mortgage Meltdown," Associated Press, March 22, 2007.
12. Gretchen Morgenson and Julie Creswell, "Borrowing Trouble," *New York Times*, April 1, 2007.
13. Ibid.
14. Rex Nutting, "Bernanke Sees Moderate Growth, Slower Inflation," MarketWatch, March 28, 2007, http:/www.marketwatch.com/.
15. E. Scott Reckard and Michael Hudson, "More Mortgage Lenders Targeted," *Los Angeles Times*, January 31, 2006; survey conducted by October Research Corp.
16. John W. Schoen, "The Mortgage Mess," MSNBC.com, April 10, 2007, http://www.msnbc.msn.com/id/17948160/.
17. David Cho, "Pressure at Mortgage Firm Led to Mass Approval of Bad Loans," *Washington Post*, May 7, 2007.
18. Mary Kane, "Cities Started to Feel the Pain," *Newark Star-Ledger*, March 18, 2007.
19. Mark Whitehouse, " 'Subprime' Aftermath: Losing the Family Home," *Wall Street Journal*, May 30, 2007.
20. James R. Hagerty, "Mortgage Brokers: Friends or Foes?" *Wall Street Journal*, May 24, 2007.
21. Michael Hudson, "How Wall Street Stoked the Mortgage Meltdown," *Wall Street Journal*, June 27, 2007.
22. Carrick Mollenkamp, "HSBC Cleans House at Mortgage Subsidiary," *Globe and Mail*, February 23, 2007.
23. Larry Bewley, "NANCE Companies Help High-Risk Borrowers," *News & Record*, June 23, 1999.
24. Robert G. Quercia, Michael A. Stegman, and Walter R. Davis, *The Impact of North Carolina's Anti-Predatory Lending Law: A Descriptive Assessment*, Center for Community Capitalism, University of North Carolina at Chapel Hill, June 25, 2003.
25. Linda Greenhouse, "Ruling Limits State Control of Big Banks," *New York Times*, April 18, 2007.

6: THE DEBT-FOR-DIPLOMA SYSTEM

1. Mark Johnson, "New York's Attorney General Accuses Colleges, Lenders of Gouging Students on Loans," Associated Press, March 16, 2007.

2. Karen W. Arenson, "Columbia to Pay $1.1 Million to State Fund in Loan Scandal," *New York Times*, June 1, 2007; Karen W. Arenson and Diana Jean Schemo, "Senate Report Details Deals in Student Loan Industry," *New York Times*, June 15, 2007.

3. Johnson, "New York's Attorney General Accuses Colleges."

4. Project on Student Debt, "Quick Facts About Student Debt," 2007, http://projectonstudentdebt.org/files/File/Debt_Facts_and_Sources _5_4_07.pdf.

5. Mary Beth Marklein, "Costs Keep Students from First-Choice Colleges," *USA Today*, January 19, 2007.

6. Demos, *Higher and Higher Education: Trends in Access, Affordability and Debt*, Winter 2007, p. 4.

7. Nancy Hoffman, "College Credit in High School: Increasing College Attainment Rates for Underrepresented Students," *Change*, July/August 2003.

8. *Empty Promises: The Myth of College Access in America*, Advisory Committee on Student Financial Assistance report, June 2002.

9. Demos, *Higher and Higher Education*, p. 4.

10. Tamara Draut, *Strapped: Why America's 20- and 30-Somethings Can't Get Ahead* (New York: Doubleday, 2006).

11. Robert Lowe, "The GI Bill Doesn't Vouch for Vouchers," *Rethinking Schools* 9, no. 4 (Summer 1995), http://www.rethinkingschools .org/special_reports/voucher_report/vgibill.shtml.

12. College Board, "Trends in Student Aid 2006" and "Trends in College Pricing 2006," http://www.collegeboard.com.

13. Edward Humes, "U.S. Future Needs 'Right Thing'—a GI Bill Resurrection," *Salt Lake City Deseret News*, October 28, 2006.

14. The GI bill cost $5.5 billion per year over seven years; adjustment for inflation brings the annual amount to $13 billion per year. See Paul Simon, "A GI Bill for Today," *Chronicle of Higher Education*, October 31, 2003, http://chronicle.com/free/v50/i10/10b01601.htm.

15. Arthur Levine and Jana Nidiffer, *Beating the Odds: How the Poor Get to College* (San Francisco: Jossey-Bass, 1996), p. 35.
16. Anya Kamanetz, *Generation Debt: Why Now Is a Terrible Time to Be Young* (New York: Riverhead, 2006), p. 15.
17. College Board, "Trends in College Pricing 2006."
18. State Higher Education Executive Officers, *State Higher Education Finance, FY 2005, Executive Overview*, April 2006, www.sheeo.org.
19. College Board, "Trends in College Pricing 2006."
20. Project on Student Debt, "Quick Facts About Student Debt."
21. Draut, *Strapped.*
22. College Board, "Trends in Student Aid 2006."
23. Diana Jean Schemo, "Congress Passes Overhaul of Student Aid Programs," *New York Times*, September 8, 2007.
24. Kati Haycock, *Promise Abandoned: How Policy Choices and Institutional Practices Restrict College Opportunities*, Education Trust, August 2006, http://www2.edtrust.org/EdTrust/Promise+Abandoned+Report.htm.
25. Ibid.
26. Elizabeth F. Farrell, "Public Colleges Tame Costs of Tuition," *Chronicle of Higher Education*, October 28, 2005.
27. Ibid.
28. Thomas R. Wolanin, ed., *Reauthorizing the Higher Education Act: Issues and Options* (Washington, DC: Institute for Higher Education Policy, 2003).
29. *Access Denied: Restoring the Nation's Commitment to Equal Educational Opportunity*, Advisory Committee on Student Financial Aid Assistance report, February 2001.
30. Deanne Loonin, *No Way Out: Student Loans, Financial Distress, and the Need for Policy Reform*, National Consumer Law Center, June 2006, http://www.consumerlaw.org.
31. Ibid.
32. National Center for Education Statistics, "Debt Burden of College Graduates," March 2005, http://nces.ed.gov.
33. Sandy Baum and Marie O'Malley, "College on Credit: How Borrowers Perceive Their Education Debt; Results of the 2002 National Stu-

dent Loan Survey," Nellie Mae Corporation, February 6, 2003, http://www.nelliemae.com/library/research_10.html; Jon Gertner, "Forgive Us Our Student Debts," *New York Times*, June 11, 2006.

34. Gertner, "Forgive Us."
35. ABA Commission on Loan Repayment and Forgiveness, *Lifting the Burden: Law Student Debt as a Barrier to Public Service*, American Bar Association, 2003, http://www.abanet.org/legalservices/down loads/lrap/lrapfinalreport.pdf.
36. College Board, "Trends in Student Aid 2006," table 7a.
37. Michael Dannenberg, "Private Loans," Higher Ed Watch Blog, February 15, 2007, http://www.newamerica.net/programs/education _policy/higher_ed_watch/blog.
38. College Board, "Trends in Student Aid 2006," table 1.
39. College Board, "Students Relying More Heavily on Private Lenders," October 2006, http://www.collegeboard.com/.
40. Office of Management and Budget, *Budget of the United States Government: Appendix Fiscal Year 2008*, http://origin.www.gpoaccess .gov/usbudget/fy08/browse.html.
41. Committee on Education and the Workforce, "Bipartisan Student Loan Bill Would Boost Funding for College Scholarships by $12 Billion Without Costing Taxpayers a Dime, Says CBO," news release, January 12, 2005, http://www.house.gov/apps/list/press/edlabor_dem/ pr_050112_studentloan.html.
42. Madeleine May Kunin, "A Math Lesson on College Loans," *New York Times*, June 13, 2007.
43. "Federal Government Relations Strategy Discussion," internal Sallie Mae strategy document, December 5, 2006, http://www.new america.net/files/SLM_Strategy_Document.pdf.

7: STICKING IT TO THE SICK

1. Peggie Sherry interview by Cindy Zeldin; testimony at *Borrowing to Stay Healthy* press conference, January 16, 2006.
2. National Health Expenditure Data, Centers for Medicare and Medicaid Services, Office of the Actuary, U.S. Department of Health and

Human Services, http://www.cms.hhs.gov/NationalHealthExpend Data/.

3. Robert B. Helms, "Tax Reform and Health Insurance," Health Policy Outlook, American Enterprise Institute, January 1, 2005, http://www.aei.org/.

4. U.S. Census Bureau, "Historical Health Insurance Tables," table HI-1, "Health Insurance Coverage Status and Type of Coverage by Sex, Race and Hispanic Origin: 1987 to 2005," http://www.census.gov; U.S. Census Bureau, "Household Income Rises, Poverty Rate Declines, Number of Uninsured Up," news release, August 28, 2007.

5. Sara R. Collins, Karen Davis, Michelle M. Doty, Jennifer L. Kriss, and Alyssa L. Holmgren, *Gaps in Health Insurance: An All-American Problem*, Commonwealth Fund, April 2006, http://www.cmwf.org/.

6. Bureau of Labor Statistics, "Median Years of Tenure with Current Employer for Employed Wage and Salary Workers by Age and Sex, Selected Years, 1996–2006," Employee Tenures Statistics, U.S. Department of Labor, September 8, 2006.

7. Carol Pryor, Andrew Cohen, and Jeffrey Prottas, *The Illusion of Coverage: How Health Insurance Fails People When They Get Sick*, Access Project, 2007, http://www.accessproject.org/.

8. Kaiser Family Foundation and Health Research and Educational Trust, "Employer Health Benefits: 2006 Annual Survey," 2006, http://www.kff.org/insurance/7527/index.cfm.

9. Ibid.

10. Michelle M. Doty, Jennifer N. Edwards, and Alyssa L. Holmgren, "Seeing Red: Americans Driven into Debt by Medical Bills: Results from a National Survey," issue brief, Commonwealth Fund, August 2005, http://www.commonwealthfund.org/.

11. Malcolm Gladwell, "The Moral Hazard Myth," *New Yorker*, August 29, 2005.

12. RAND, "The Health Insurance Experiment: A Classic RAND Study Speaks to the Current Health Care Reform Debate," RAND Health Research Highlights, 2006.

13. "Healthy? Insurers Don't Buy It; Minor Ailments Can Thwart Applicants for Individual Policies," *Los Angeles Times*, December 31, 2006.

14. Ibid.

15. Kaiser Daily Health Report, "Health Insurance Premium Rates Increase Faster Than Income, Study Says," October 18, 2006, http://www.kaisernetwork.org.

16. Ha T. Tu, "Rising Health Costs, Medical Debt and Chronic Conditions," Issue Brief No. 88, Center for Studying Health System Change, September 2004, http://www.hschange.org/CONTENT/706/.

17. Pryor, Cohen, and Prottas, *Illusion of Coverage*.

18. Cindy Zeldin and Mark Rukavina, *Borrowing to Stay Healthy: How Credit Card Debt Is Related to Medical Expenses*, Demos and the Access Project, January 2007.

19. Kaiser Commission on Medicaid and the Uninsured, *The Uninsured: A Primer*, Kaiser Family Foundation, October 2006.

20. Lucette Lagnado, "Hospitals Try Extreme Measures to Collect Their Overdue Debts: Patients Who Skip Hearings on Bills Are Arrested; It's a 'Body Attachment,' " *Wall Street Journal*, October 30, 2003.

21. Lucette Lagnado, "Anatomy of a Hospital Bill: Uninsured Patients Often Face Big Markups on Small Items; 'Rules are Completely Crazy,' " *Wall Street Journal*, September 21, 2004.

22. Andrea B. Staiti, Robert E. Hurley, and Peter J. Cunningham, "Balancing Margin and Mission: Hospitals Alter Billing and Collection Practices for Uninsured Patients," Issue Brief No. 99, Center for Studying Health System Change, October 2005, http://www.hschange.com/CONTENT/788/.

23. Carol Pryor, "The Hospital Billing and Collections Flap: It's Not Over Yet," *Journal of Health Care Compliance*, May/June 2005.

24. Families USA, "A Pound of Flesh: Hospital Billing, Debt Collection, and Patients' Rights," Issue Brief, March 2007, http://www.familiesusa.org/.

25. Zeldin and Rukavina, *Borrowing to Stay Healthy*.

26. Access Project, *The Consequences of Medical Debt: Evidence from Three Communities*, February 2003, http://www.accessproject.org/.

27. Eben Fetters and Ron Luke, "Get Paid Now: Enhance Your Hospital's Margins by Collecting Co-pays and Deductibles," Health Leaders Media, October 2006; Subcommittee on Oversight and Investigations, House Committee on Energy and Commerce, "A Review of Hospital Billing and Collections Practices," witness testimonies of Melissa Jacoby and Mark Rukavina, June 24, 2004; Access Project, *Consequences of Medical Debt.*

28. Demos and Center for Responsible Lending, *The Plastic Safety Net: The Reality Behind Debt in America,* October 2005.

29. Zeldin and Rukavina, *Borrowing to Stay Healthy.*

30. For a detailed analysis of credit card fees, see U.S. Government Accountability Office, *Credit Cards: Increased Complexity in Rates and Fees Heightens Need for More Effective Disclosures to Consumers,* Report to the Ranking Minority Member, Permanent Subcommittee on Investigations, Committee on Homeland Security and Governmental Affairs, U.S. Senate, GAO-06-929, September 2006, http://www.gao.gov/.

31. Christopher Rowland, "Patients Piling Medical Costs on Credit Cards," *Boston Globe,* January 22, 2007.

32. Robert W. Seifert, *Home Sick: How Medical Debt Undermines Housing Security,* Access Project, November 2005, http://www.access project.org/.

33. David U. Himmelstein, Elizabeth Warren, Deborah Thorne, and Steffie Woolhander, "Illness and Injury as Contributors to Bankruptcy," *Health Affairs,* February 2, 2005, http://www.health affairs.org/.

34. Catherine Hoffman, Diane Rowland, and Elizabeth C. Hamel, "Medical Debt and Access to Care," Kaiser Family Foundation, September 2005, http://www.kff.org.

35. Eric Brunner, "Socioeconomic Determinants of Health; Stress and the Biology of Inequality," *British Medical Journal* 314, no. 7092 (May 17, 1997), pp. 1472–76; Michael Marmot, "Historical Perspective: The Social Determinants of Disease—Some Blossoms," *Epidemiologic Perspectives and Innovations* 2, no. 4 (2005).

36. Daniel Costello, "Hospital Bills—But with Interest; Now Patients

Who Can't Pay, or Who Have High Deductibles, Can Get Credit Cards Specifically for Medical Care. But the Rates Can Reach 23%," *Los Angeles Times*, December 12, 2005. See also Melissa Jacoby, "Hospital Bad Debt and Medical Credit Cards," Credit Slips, July 2006, http://www.creditslips.org/creditslips/2006/07/hospital_bad_de.html.

37. Mike Stobbe, "Credit Card Agency Cuts Hospitals' Losses," *Charlotte Observer*, July 11, 2003.

38. Leslie A. Pappas, "More and More Medical Bills Paid on Credit," *Wilmington News Journal*, January 17, 2007.

8: THE McSHARKS

1. Robert W. Johnson and Dixie P. Johnson, *Pawnbroking in the U.S.: A Profile of Customers*, Georgetown University Credit Research Center, 1998, http://www.business.gwu.edu.

2. Ibid.

3. "Alicia Alvarez" interview by James Lardner, July 17, 2007.

4. Sue Kirchhoff, "Some Lenders Run into Big Problems with Auto Title Lending," *USA Today*, December 26, 2006.

5. Ibid.

6. Howard Karger, *Shortchanged: Life and Debt in the Fringe Economy* (San Francisco: Berrett-Koehler, 2005).

7. "Alicia Alvarez" interview.

8. Brian Grow and Keith Epstein, "The Poverty Business," *Business-Week*, May 21, 2007.

9. James M. Lacko, Signe-Mary McKernan, and Manoj Hastak, "Survey of Rent-to-Own Customers," Bureau of Economics staff report, Federal Trade Commission, July 2001.

10. Jay MacDonald, "Refund-Anticipation Loans Can Carry a High Price," Bankrate.com, March 15, 2006, http://www.bankrate.com/brm/itax/news/20030127a1.asp.

11. Chi Chi Wu, Jean Ann Fox, and Elizabeth Renuart, "Refund Anticipation Loan Report," Consumer Federation of America and the National Consumer Law Center, 2002, http://www.nclc.org; Grow and Epstein, "Poverty Business."

12. MacDonald, "Refund-Anticipation Loans."

13. Jean Ann Fox, Patrick Woodall, and Chi Chi Wu, "Another Year of Losses: High-Priced Refund Anticipation Loans Continue to Take a Chunk Out of Americans' Tax Refunds," National Consumer Law Center and Consumer Federation of America, January 2006.

14. Noah Sawyer and Kenneth Temkin, "Analysis of Alternative Financial Services Providers," Fannie Mae Foundation, February 2004.

15. Advance America Web site, http://advanceamerica.net/.

16. Christopher Conkey, "Payday Lenders Strike a Defensive Pose," *Wall Street Journal*, February 21, 2007.

17. Karger, *Shortchanged*; Grow and Epstein, "Poverty Business."

18. Sawyer and Temkin, "Alternative Financial Service Providers."

19. Ibid.

20. Karger, *Shortchanged*.

21. See http://advanceamerica.net/mythvsreality.php.

22. Grow and Epstein, "Poverty Business."

23. Uriah King, Leslie Parrish, and Ozlem Tanik, "Financial Quicksand," Center for Responsible Lending, November 30, 2006, http://www.responsiblelending.org/.

24. Alejandro Gonzalez, "SOS: Trapped in Payday Loans," *USA Today*, October 2, 2006.

25. King, Parrish, and Tanik, "Financial Quicksand."

26. Consumer Credit Division, Illinois Department of Financial and Professional Regulation, "Short-Term Lending Final Report," n.d., p. 26, http://www.idfpr.com/.

27. King, Parrish, and Tanik, "Financial Quicksand."

28. Ibid.

29. Hoover's Fact Sheet, "Cash America International, Inc.," April 2007, http://www.hoovers.com/.

30. Hoover's Fact Sheet, "EZCORP, Inc.," April 2007, http://www.hoovers.com/.

31. Grow and Epstein, "Poverty Business."

32. William C. Apgar Jr. and Herbert E. Christopher, *Subprime Lending and Alternative Financial Service Providers: A Literature Review and Empirical Analysis*, Office of Policy Development and Research, U.S.

Department of Housing and Urban Development, February 2006, p. 186, http://www.huduser.org/.

33. ACE Cash Express, *ACE Community Fund Annual Report*, 2005.

34. Anne Kim, "The Unbanked and the Alternative Financial Sector," Progressive Policy Institute, April 5, 2001, http://www.ppionline.org/.

35. MSN Money, "Advance America, Cash Advance Centers, Inc.," MSN Fact Sheet, August 2007, http://moneycentral.hoovers.com/global/msn/factsheet.xhtml?COID=113066.

36. Mark S. Gottlieb, "Check Cashing: An Industry Study," MSG Accountants, Consultants, and Business Valuators, 2006, http://www.msgcpa.com/; Edward Robinson, "JPMorgan, Banks Back Lenders Luring Poor with 780 Percent Rates," Bloomberg.com, November 23, 2004; Warren Bolton, "Banks Supply Cash That Fuels Payday Lenders' Astronomical Growth," TheState.com, June 2007.

37. U.S. Public Interest Research Group, "Rent-a-Bank Payday Lending: How Banks Help Payday Lenders Evade State Consumer Protections," November 11, 2001, http://www.uspirg.org/.

38. Chris Cuomo, Mary Harris, and Lara Sketrankian, "Are Predatory Lenders Ripping Off Our Nation's Finest?" Law & Justice Unit, ABC News, August 22, 2006.

39. Elizabeth Dole, "Taking Aim at Our Military; Congress Should Provide Protection Against Predatory Payday Lenders," *Charlotte Observer*, September 18, 2006; Rick Rogers, "Military Has Payday Loans in Its Sights; Service Members Called Vulnerable," *San Diego Union Tribune*, May 23, 2006.

40. Advance America Web site.

41. Community Financial Services Association, "Payday Advance Companies Give Back to Communities," http://www.cfsa.net/giving_back_to_communities.html.

42. Susan Orr, "Billy Webster: A Man of Achievement," *Spartanburg Herald*, July 3, 2005.

43. Community Financial Services Association of America, "Payday Advance Industry Implements First Stage of Changes to Educate and Protect Consumers Nationwide," news release, May 31, 2007, http://www.cfsa.net/.

44. Advance America, "Lawmakers Vote to Maintain Payday Lending in Virginia," news release, December 5, 2006, http://investors.advance america.net/releasedetail.cfm?ReleaseID=220970.
45. King, Parrish, and Tanik, "Financial Quicksand."
46. Sawyer and Temkin, "Alternative Financial Service Providers."
47. Apgar and Christopher, "Subprime Lending."
48. Uriah King, Wei Li, Delvin Davis, and Keith Ernst, *Race Matters: The Concentration of Payday Lenders in African-American Neighborhoods in North Carolina*, research report, Center for Responsible Lending, March 22, 2005, http://www.responsiblelending.org.
49. Alan Fisher, "The Financial Divide: An Uneven Playing Field: Bank Financing of Check Cashers and Payday Lenders in California Communities," California Reinvestment Coalition, March 2005, http:// www.calreinvest.org.
50. Michelle Singletary, "Payday Loan Companies Unsavory, but Very Savvy," *Washington Post*, February 24, 2007.
51. Grow and Epstein, "Poverty Business."
52. Anne Kim, *The Unbanked and the Alternative Financial Sector*, Federal Reserve Bank of Chicago, April 5, 2001.

9: THE END OF THE ROPE

1. Beth Healy and Walter V. Robinson, "Regulators, Policy Makers Seldom Intervene," *Boston Globe*, August 2, 2006.
2. Ibid.
3. ACA International, "Industry Statistics: Collection Facts," January 15, 2007, http://www.acainternational.org/.
4. Caroline E. Mayer, "As Debt Collectors Multiply, So Do Consumer Complaints," *Washington Post*, July 28, 2005.
5. Ibid.
6. Healy and Robinson, "Regulators."
7. Figure for number of complaints filed in 2005 from "Federal Trade Commission Annual Report 2006: Fair Debt Collection Practices Act"; figure for 2000 complaints from Mayer, "As Debt Collectors Multiply."
8. Ibid.

9. Sewell Chan, "An Outcry Rises as Debt Collectors Play Rough," *New York Times*, July 5, 2006.

10. Healy and Robinson, "Regulators."

11. "Debt Collection Puts on a Suit," *BusinessWeek*, November 14, 2005.

12. Marilyn Lewis, "New IRS Tactic: Private Debt Collectors," MSN Money.com, http://articles.moneycentral.msn.com/Taxes/CutYour Taxes/NewIRSTacticPrivateDebtCollectors.aspx?page=all.

13. U.S. Senate Committee on Homeland Security and Governmental Affairs, *Profiteering in a Non-profit Industry: Abusive Practices in Credit Counseling* (Washington, DC: U.S. Government Printing Office, 2005).

14. Deanne Loonin and Travis Plunkett, *Credit Counseling in Crisis: The Impact on Consumers of Funding Cuts, Higher Fees and Aggressive New Market Entrants*, Consumer Federation of America and National Consumer Law Center, April 2003, http://www.consumer fed.org/pdfs/credit_counseling_report.pdf.

15. ConsumerAffairs.com, "Solidium Credit Recovery Services," May 18, 2004, http://www.consumeraffairs.com/debt_counsel/solidium .html.

16. Ibid.

17. ConsumerAffairs.com, "Court Closes National Consumer Council," May 5, 2004, http://www.consumeraffairs.com/news04/national _consumer.html.

18. Caroline E. Mayer, "AmeriDebt Founder Faces Trial Next Week," *Washington Post*, January 2, 2006.

19. "AmeriDebt Sued for Fraud," CBSNews.com, September 12, 2003, http://www.cbsnews.com/stories/2003/11/19/national/main584546 .shtml.

20. Caroline E. Mayer, "Easing the Credit Crunch," *Washington Post*, November 4, 2001.

21. U.S. Senate Committee on Homeland Security and Governmental Affairs, *Profiteering in a Non-Profit Industry*.

22. Mayer, "AmeriDebt Founder Faces Trial."

23. Federal Trade Commission, "AmeriDebt Founder Settles FTC Deception Charges," news release, September 13, 2006.

24. Patricia Sabatini, "IRS Slams Credit Counseling Agencies," *Pittsburgh Post-Gazette*, May 16, 2006.

25. American Bankruptcy Institute, "U.S. Business and Non-Business Bankruptcy Filings, 1980–2006," http://www.abiworld.org/Content/ NavigationMenu/NewsRoom/BankruptcyStatistics/Bankruptcy _Filings_1.htm.

26. U.S. Government Accountability Office, *Credit Cards: Increased Complexity in Rates and Fees Heightens Need for More Effective Disclosures to Consumers*, Report to the Ranking Minority Member, Permanent Subcommittee on Investigations, Committee on Homeland Security and Governmental Affairs, U.S. Senate, GAO-06-929, September 2006, p. 9, http://www.gao.gov/.

27. See Lawrence M. Ausubel, "Credit Card Defaults, Credit Card Profits, and Bankruptcy," *American Bankruptcy Law Journal* 71 (1997); and Ronald Mann, "Cards, Consumer Credit and Bankruptcy," paper 36, American Law and Economics Association Annual Meetings, 2006, http://law.bepress.com/cgi/viewcontent.cgi?article=1853 &context=alea.

28. See David U. Himmelstein, Deborah Thorne, Elizabeth Warren, and Steffie Woolhandler, "Illness and Injury as Contributors to Bankruptcy," *Health Affairs*, February 5, 2005, http://content.healthaffairs .org/cgi/content/full/hlthaff.w5.63/DC1; and Elizabeth Warren and Amelia Warren Tyagi, *The Two-Income Trap: Why Middle Class Mothers and Fathers Are Going Broke* (New York: Basic Books, 2003).

29. See Warren and Tyagi, *Two-Income Trap*.

30. Ibid.

31. Brigitte Yuille, "Bankruptcy Law Still Controversial 1 Year Later," Bankrate.com, October 17, 2006, http://www.bankrate.com/brm/ news/bankruptcy/Oct06_bankruptcy_law_anniversary_a1.asp.

32. Bankruptcy reform legislation had been under consideration for about eight years before its final passage. It began with House Bill 2500 in the 105th Congress (1997).

33. Stephen Labaton, "Bankruptcy Bill Set for Passage; Victory for Bush," *New York Times*, March 9, 2005.

34. House Judiciary Committee, "Committee Approves Senate-Passed

Bankruptcy Reform Legislation Without Amendment," news release, March 16, 2006, p. 1, http://judiciary.house.gov/.

35. Labaton, "Bankruptcy Bill Set for Passage."

36. American Bankruptcy Institute, "Annual Non-Business Filings By Chapter, 2000–2006," http://www.abiworld.org/Content/Navigation Menu/NewsRoom/BankruptcyStatistics/Bankruptcy_Filings_1.htm.

37. Consumer Bankruptcy News, "Filing Drought Is About Over," October 12, 2006.

38. National Association of Consumer Bankruptcy Attorneys, "Bankruptcy Reform's Impact: Where Are All the Deadbeats?" February 22, 2006, http://www.nacba.org.

39. Dan Frosch, "Your Money or Your Life," *The Nation*, February 3, 2005.

10: ADDRESSING THE DEBT CRISIS

1. Federal Reserve Board, "Household Debt Service and Financial Obligations Ratios," statistical release, http://www.federalreserve.gov/Releases/housedebt/.

2. See Americans for Fairness in Lending Web site, http://www.affil.org/. Demos is a partner in the Americans for Fairness in Lending coalition.

3. U.S. Senate Permanent Subcommittee on Investigations, Committee on Homeland Security and Governmental Affairs, Hearing on "Credit Card Practices: Fees, Interest Rates, and Grace Periods," March 7, 2007.

4. Ozlem Tanik, "Payday Lenders Target the Military," CRL Issue Paper No. 11, Center for Responsible Lending, September 29, 2005.

5. Ellen Schloemer, Wei Li, Keith Ernst, and Kathleen Keest, *Losing Ground: Foreclosures in the Subprime Market and Their Cost to Homeowners*, Center for Responsible Lending, December 2006, http://www.responsiblelending.org/.

6. Brian Grow and Keith Epstein, "The Poverty Business," *BusinessWeek*, May 21, 2007.

7. Elizabeth Warren, "Unsafe at Any Rate," *Democracy: A Journal of Ideas*, no. 5 (Summer 2007).

8. Ruth Simon and James R. Hagerty, "Mortgage Mess Shines Light on Brokers' Role," *Wall Street Journal*, July 5, 2007.

9. Lillian Woo and David Buchholz, "Subsidies for Assets: A New Look at the Federal Budget," Corporation for Enterprise Development, February 2007, http://www.cfed.org/.

10. Ray Boshara, Reid Cramer, and Rourke O'Brien, "The Assets Agenda 2007," New America Foundation, April 2007, http://www.new america.net/.

11. See America Saves Web site, http://www.americasaves.org/.

12. Sue Kirchhoff, "Breaking the Cycle of Payday Loan 'Trap,' " *USA Today*, September 19, 2006.

13. Tamara Draut, *Strapped: Why America's 20- and 30-Somethings Can't Get Ahead* (New York: Doubleday, 2006).

14. Matt Fellowes, *From Poverty, Opportunity: Putting the Market to Work for Low-Income Families*, Brookings Institution, July 2006.

15. Elizabeth Warren and Amelia Warren Tyagi, *The Two-Income Trap: Why Middle Class Mothers and Fathers Are Going Broke* (New York: Basic Books, 2003), pp. 51–52.

16. For a detailed description of the Contract for College, see David Callahan, Tamara Draut, and Javier Silva, *Millions to the Middle: Three Strategies to Expand the Middle Class*, Demos, 2004.

17. Ballot Initiative Strategy Center, "The 2006 Initiative and Referenda Election Results," November 2006, http://www.ballot.org/.

18. Bureau of Labor Statistics, "Union Members in 2006," news release, January 25, 2007.

19. Dale Russakoff, "Bill Easing Organization of Unions Passes House," *Washington Post*, March 2, 2007.

ACKNOWLEDGMENTS

Three authors might sound like plenty, but we truly could not have written this book by ourselves.

The idea was Ellen Adler's. It was Ellen, speaking for The New Press, who infected Miles Rapoport with her enthusiasm for a book about debt. It was Miles who convinced us to accept this assignment on top of what we foolishly thought was a full plate of other responsibilities. Now that the book is finished, we can thank him for that. We also thank Miles for his large role in making Demos a place where the three of us (among others) have been able to do work we care about deeply.

Tamara Draut's help was continuous and invaluable. Long before we embarked on this project, she was the driving force behind Demos's debt work, building a base of knowledge that was our starting point. At the outset, Tammy helped us organize the territory into topics and themes, and pointed us to crucial sources of information. Then she served as our field marshal, handing out missions ("Zeldin—you take medical debt," "García—deregulation," etc.) and making sure we performed them on schedule.

Because the schedule was tight and the subject large and complicated, we leaned heavily on many colleagues. Myra Batchelder, Gennady Kolker, and Jennifer Wheary were very important to this enterprise; all, at times, engaged in activities not easily distinguished from those of an "author." We thank a former colleague,

Javier Silva, for his contributions to many excellent Demos reports involving debt and the lending industry.

Our work was helped immeasurably by the efforts of a number of public-interest groups that have worked valiantly on these issues: the Access Project, ACORN, the Center for Responsible Lending, Consumer Action, Consumers Union, the Consumer Federation of America, the National Consumer Law Center, the Project on Student Debt, and U.S. PIRG, to name a few. We also thank Elizabeth Warren and Amelia Warren Tyagi, who, in their writing and advocacy, have almost been an organization unto themselves.

We are grateful to Elizabeth Renuart of the National Consumer Law Center for steering us through the maze of lending deregulation and passing her expert eye over an early draft of that chapter. Mary Moore of the Center for Responsible Lending performed a similar service with the two chapters on home equity loans and the subprime mortgage industry (although, of course, any remaining mistakes are our own). For other acts of assistance, we thank Jordan Ash, Jonathan Cohn, Nancy Register, and Mark Rukavina.

On this second publishing alliance between Demos and The New Press, Ellen Adler and her colleagues—including Sarah Fan, Jyothi Natarajan, and Joseph Huff-Hannon—began to seem like old buddies. Nice working with you all. Thanks also to Leon Friedman for steering us clear (we hope) of any legal offenses.

José García thanks his wife, Lili, for her patience, her nurturing support, and her insightful edits as she read sections of the manuscript. Cindy Zeldin thanks her husband, Doug Busk, for his encouragement and thoughtful feedback.

Finally, we thank all the people who directly or indirectly contributed their personal stories to this narrative. We are especially grateful to Peggie Sherry, Alfonso Ynigues, Jeffrey Williams, and "Alicia Alvarez" and "Michael Alvarez" for their help in describing their debt-related heartaches and misadventures.